ENDORSEMENT

I first met Dawn in 2021 when she came along to one of my Arise Sanctuary retreats in Noosa. During that time, God stirred something in her heart and planted the seed for her very first book, Hope Faith Truth.

Since then, I've known Dawn as someone who continually encourages others—quick to pray, quick to speak life, and always pointing people back to God. Through her writing and her Hope Faith Truth page, she faithfully uses her gifts to glorify Him and bless those around her.

Dawn carries such a deep compassion for women. She has a beautiful way of walking alongside others through both the highs and the challenges of life, gently reminding them of the hope we have in Him.

It's such a joy to see her step into this new season and release her fourth book. My prayer is that God would richly bless her and that this book will continue to bring encouragement and truth to many.

Lisa Bruton
Director Arise Sanctuary

The Journey

Dawn Pryor

Ark House Press
arkhousepress.com

Cataloguing in Publication Data:
Title: The Journey
ISBN: 978-1-7643052-3-5 (pbk)
Subjects: [REL012020]   RELIGION / Christian Living / Devotional; [REL012120] RELIGION / Christian Living / Spiritual Growth; [REL012130]   RELIGION / Christian Living / Women's Interests.

Design by initiateagency.com

CONTENTS

The Journey

Isaiah 58:11 (NLT)
The Lord will guide you continually, giving you water when
you are dry, and restoring your strength. You will be like a
well-watered garden, like an ever-flowing spring.

From the moment we are born, until we take our last breath, we are all on a journey. Some steps on our journey we take alone, and some steps we take with others, but every step we take, we take with God.

All of us have hopes, dreams and plans, we have things we want to do with our lives, adventures we want to take. However, the best laid plans can often go astray, things happen, life gets in the way and suddenly all we thought was ours for the taking just disappears before our eyes.

No one knew this better than Joseph. He had a dream, God showed him that he would become a great man in his nation, that many would look up to him and he would have power and authority throughout the land. But, before any of this came to pass, Joseph walked a long and arduous journey, a journey that none of us would choose to take. He suffered greatly at the hands of others, firstly those who called themselves his brothers, and then seemingly, by every other person he met.

On our journey there are many things that can overwhelm us, that can beat us down, and life can look very different to what we thought it would. All our hopes and plans can be dashed in a moment, and everything we thought we knew can be stripped away.

It is there, in that place, in the darkness, when nothing is what we thought it would be, when heartache comes, and life suddenly stands still, it is in this moment, we cry out to God. He is our refuge, our strong tower, our mountain, our only hope. It is when we are at the crossroads, when the path is going nowhere, when we run out of road, and our journey seems to have taken us off the beaten track, it's here that God steps in to guide us, refresh us, and restore our strength.

If the journey that you're on today isn't what you thought it would be, don't give up, hold tight to God and allow Him to walk with you, let Him restore your strength and carry you until you're ready to keep going. Let Him be the One who orders your steps and guides your way.

Prayer

Lord, I thank you that you are with me on the journey of life, that each step I take is with you, that you are leading me and guiding me everywhere I go.

Lord, on the days when life feels too hard, when I can't put one foot in front of the other, thank you for being my strength, for carrying me when I am too weak to keep going.

God, I pray for your refreshment, that you would infuse my tired and weary bones, that you would fill me to overflowing, and that I would find my hope in you.

As I face a new day, and it looks different to what I was expecting, help me to continue to trust in you, not giving in to doubt and confusion, but instead, relying on you for all that I need.

I pray you walk with me through disappointment, through heartbreak and despair, and that you would be my hiding place when the darkness tries to consume me.

Lord there is no one I would rather be with as I face each day, walk with me now I pray.

Amen.

Seasons

Ecclesiastes 3:1 (NIV)
There is a time for everything, and a season
for every activity under the heavens.

For each of us there are seasons that bring us joy, and then there are seasons that bring us heartache. We don't get to choose what season we are in; we don't have the monopoly on all the good times, without the bad.

Like most, I have walked through many seasons that have been hard, seasons that I wouldn't have chosen for myself. There have been days where I thought I would drown in my own tears and have struggled to face the morning after the long night before.

And equally there have been seasons of unspeakable happiness, the times where I have felt that my heart would burst, and my face has literally hurt from smiling. Seasons that have truly been perfect rays of sunshine, where I have felt that all was well with the world.

In all these seasons, there is one thing that is constant, and that is God. He is with us on our best days, and on our worst. He is with us when we are at our lowest, and when we are on a high. He journeys with us, regardless of the season we are in.

God doesn't stop us from walking through hard days, but He walks through them with us. He holds us when we can't stand on our own, and when we can't go any further, He carries us. Likewise, on our best days He is there beside us, cheering us on, encouraging us, reminding us of how far we've come and how proud He is of us.

Just as our gardens change with the elements, so do our lives. We need to be prepared for all that life throws at us, and sometimes that can be hard. How do we prepare for the hard days? By staying close to God, by spending time with Him, by getting to know His character. In doing this we know that we can rely on Him, we know that we can trust Him, we know that when everyone else walks away, He won't. When we spend time with God, we get to know who He is, and in doing so we align ourselves with Him.

Today, no matter what season you may be in, remember that you are not in it alone, God is with you. He is rejoicing with you in your good times and holding you in your hard times. Let that be all you need today.

Prayer

Lord, I thank you that you are with me in every season, that no matter what I walk through, you walk with me.

Thank you for being my constant, for standing with me when everyone else has walked away.

Thank you that on my good days, my bad days, and on every day in between, you have held me close, reminding me of who I am, but more importantly, for reminding me of who you are.

God, let me never take for granted who you are in my life but let me always remember that you are my everything. You are the one who goes before me, who stands beside me, and who surrounds me. You are with me in the battle, and you are with me in the triumph, you are the One who is my all in all.

Holy Spirit, speak into my heart, that on the days when I can't find my place, when my feet are on shaky ground, and when all I thought was mine to hold is taken away, remind me, that this is just for a season, and it too shall pass.

Thank you, Lord Jesus, that in this season, you are my portion, and that is more than enough.

Amen

Commit Your Way

God wants us to enjoy life, and to be fulfilled, He wants us to be healthy and prosperous. But the one thing He wants most of all, is for us to be wholly committed to Him, to place our lives in His hands and for us to stand on His truth.

The world would have us believe, and I think we sometimes let ourselves fall for the lie, that God is trying to control us, that He is like some big brother in the sky who wants to intimidate us into doing all that He wants us to do. This couldn't be further from the truth, it is never God's intention to rule our lives, if it was, He would never have given us free will.

God wants us to work with Him, to follow in His ways, to place our trust in Him, and have faith because of Him. He sees the bigger picture, so He ultimately knows what is best for us. Because of this He has a great roadmap for us to follow, a purpose for our journey, a plan that doesn't include us getting hurt or being sideswiped by disappointment, but a plan that is for our benefit and our good.

God wants us to have all that we desire, He wants us to have fun, to be encouraged, to enjoy our work, and to have harmony within our families. He wants us to be blessed financially, and to experience all His goodness. It is never His will to withhold from us all that we desire, and all that He asks in return is that we commit our lives and our way to Him.

My encouragement for you today is that you would allow God to be Lord of your life, that you would find your place in Him, and walk with Him through each day. Take the time to get to know Him and diligently seek Him as you go about pursuing your dreams, aligning your desires with His.

Prayer

Lord, today I give my life to you, I hand over all I am, and I ask that you would be Lord of my life.

God, work within every part of who I am, that I would become less of me and more of you. I pray that when others look at me, they would see Jesus.

Help me to lay down all my desires that I might fulfill your perfect purpose, and to remember that not everything is about me, but ultimately it is about you.

God, I ask that your will be done in me and through me, that I might shine your light everywhere I go. Let me be a beacon that radiates who you are to the world around me. May I let go of all that I cling to so that I can cling only to you.

Father, remind me that it is only because of who you are, that I can freely be all I am, all you created me to be. Help me to live from a place of purpose in you, and to share that with those around me.

Lord Jesus, today I offer you all I am, do with me as you will.
Amen.

Promises

Genesis 17:15-16 (NIV)
God also said to Abraham, "As for Sarai your wife, you are no
longer to call her Sarai; her name will be Sarah. I will bless her
and will surely give you a son by her. I will bless her so that she will
be the mother of nations; kings of peoples will come from her."

When God gives us a promise, we don't always have the benefit of knowing when that promise will be fulfilled. He doesn't always give us a timeline, or a step-by-step plan on how things will work out.

I'm sure for Sarah, waiting for God's promises to be fulfilled was a journey that was long and painful. When month after month she remained barren, without a child of her own, I'm sure she felt a heaviness in her spirit that was crushing.

As she watched her servant Hagar with the child that had been created with Abraham, I'm sure Sarah's heart ached, and her soul felt overwhelmed.

When was it going to be her turn?

When was God going to fulfil His promises and make her a mother?

Many of us have cried out to God in our own waiting. When we've waited for a pregnancy, a healing, a job, a change, or a resolution. When we've sat on the sidelines and watched the joys and successes of others while our hearts have broken, or our dreams have been crushed.

We have felt overlooked, left behind, or completely forgotten. We begin to doubt that God has a plan or a purpose for us, let alone, a promise.

But what we do in the waiting is just as important, if not more so, than the outcome of what we are waiting for. We need to wait with expectancy, with hope, with joy, and with a sense of thankfulness.

Just because the promise has not come to be yet, doesn't mean it's not coming. Just as any expectant mother must hold on, through the good and the bad, during the long months of pregnancy, she knows that when the timing is right, her joy will be complete.

Keep trusting God in your season of waiting, hold onto His promises, knowing that for you, His best is yet to come.

Prayer

Father God, I thank you that your promises for me are 'yes and amen'. That I am not waiting in vain, but that in due season you will bring them to pass.

Lord, as I think of the incredible women of the bible who had to trust you when their worlds were falling apart, women like Sarah, and Ruth, and Mary and Esther, women who held on to you during the greatest struggles of their lives. Lord if they could do it, I pray that you would equip me so that I could too.

Father, help me to remain faithful and steadfast, help me to lean into you as I wait for your promises to be fulfilled in my life. Let me learn from all those who have gone before me, those who never gave up, but remained hopeful in the face of disappointment and despair.

God, I know that you have blessings in abundance to pour out on me, and all I need to do is stay close to you, walk in your ways, and trust you in the everyday. Help me to see your purpose, and never doubt that your ways are higher than mine.

Lord Jesus, above all else, as I wait on you, let my heart be pure, and my words be filled with love.

Amen.

A Circle Of Quiet

This is such a beautiful portrayal of what God does for us. In the midst of evil, He provides a circle of quiet for those He loves.

We have been incredibly blessed because God has trained and instructed us in His Word. We know His truth and can walk forward in His ways, knowing that He is with us each step of the way, and because of this, we have no reason to fear.

Each of us go through times in our lives that are turbulent, where nothing seems to make sense, and we are surrounded by problem after problem. It's in these times that we need to take our eyes off our situation and place the focus back on God, trusting in Him that everything will work out alright.

When you think about a circle, it is perfectly round with no angles and no breaks, whatever is within that circle is enclosed there, it is perfectly safe, with nothing able to break through and destroy it.

We, in the same way, are held within the circle of God's perfect love, and it is here that He provides for us quiet, peace and restoration. It is here that we are safe from the outside world, and that all that clamours around us falls away.

God wants to hold us close to Him in times of trouble, as we journey, He wants to be our refuge and our rock, He wants to put our feet on solid ground. When we are going through turmoil, God wants to provide us with His circle of quiet.

I would encourage you today to be still and to allow the peace of God to encircle you, and to let Him quiet the noise within your heart and your mind, knowing that in all things, He is walking with you, holding you, and most importantly, loving you.

Prayer

Lord, I thank you that you are holding me in your circle of quiet, in your inner sanctum of peace, and in the place where I am safe and protected.

I am grateful that your arms are tightly wrapped around me, and I have no reason to fear, for I am fully enclosed in your embrace, and it is here that I am wholly yours.

Lord God, thank you for your peace which passes all understanding, the peace that allows me to sleep soundly knowing that you are in control. I thank you for the peace which does not fear the terror of night, for you alone are my protector.

God, I thank you that no matter what storm I walk through, no matter how turbulent life may be, you are still God, and that is enough. You hold my days in your hands, and nothing is going to happen that you don't allow.

Lord, I thank you for who you are, for you God are my all in all.

Amen

From Death To Life

Ephesians 2:6 (CEV)
God raised us from death to life with Christ Jesus, He
has given us a place beside Christ in heaven.

I recently attended the funeral of a beautiful Christian lady that I had known throughout my early Christian years. The service was a touching reflection of her faith, and the life she had lived for her family, her community, and her Saviour.

During the time of the message, the Pastor, spoke on how this lovely lady had not passed from life to death, but rather, she had passed from death to life. This was such a light bulb moment for me, I had never thought of this before, and although I had read scriptures that clearly stated this, I had not once considered the change of perspective that comes when we know that the passing of our loved ones is the celebration of them moving from death on earth to life in heaven.

We all know that our time here is limited, that our journey comes and goes in the blink of an eye, and we know that one day we will move from our earthly home to our heavenly home, where we will finally come face to face with Jesus. We too know that it's always devastating for those left behind when a last breath is taken, however, it's in reframing the narrative of what we are leaving to where we are going that changes the entire face of death. This place is not our forever home, it was never intended to be, it's simply where we wait for our next step, our new life to begin.

We all know that our days are numbered, that there will come a time when we go to meet out Maker, ready or not. As Christians, we have no need to fear this day, it is what we have trained for, it is the end of the race, and it is our time to take to the podium and hear the words 'Well done my good and faithful servant.' It is the day where we say goodbye to pain, to struggles, to suffering and to death, and we crossover into life.

Be encouraged by this today.

Prayer

Father God, I thank you that you are the giver of life. That it is your breath in us that allows us to be. It is you alone Lord who chose the day of our birth, and it is you who chooses the day we are called home.

I thank you that I need not fear the end, for that's never what it will be, it will simply be a stepping stone into my new life, a life with you. I am so grateful that I know in my heart that when I take my final breath here on earth, I will take my first breath in heaven.

God, I pray that you remind me of this when I mourn those I love, when I stand by the bedside or the graveside of those I hold dear, help me to remember that they are now alive and free, that they have passed from death to life, and they are with you.

Lord, on the days when my heart is heavy, and tears fill my eyes, may I always have a vision of your arms wrapped around those you love. May I see the Welcome Home banner, the celebrations, and the new life that is given to those who call out to you.

Father, until in heaven we meet
Amen

Who Told You That
You Were Naked?

Genesis 3:9-11 (TLB)
The Lord called out to Adam "Why are you hiding?" And Adam replied
"I heard you coming and didn't want you to see me naked. So, I Hid".
"Who told you that you were naked?" the Lord God asked.
"Have you eaten from the tree I warned you about?"

Guilt and shame will always cause us to hide from God. It will hang over us like a heavy cloak and drown us in fear.

In Genesis we read of the beautiful relationship between God and the man and woman He created. We see the garden that He placed them in, the life they led and the ideal surroundings that they were able to call home.

Yet it wasn't enough, still they wanted more, and they allowed that want to drive them to do the one thing that God had explicitly told them not to do. They were easily led to do what was wrong, and to listen to the voice of evil rather than the voice of good.

God, being all knowing, came looking for Adam and Eve in the garden, already fully aware of what they had done, He sought them out to talk to them.

And in doing so, He asked them one very important question.

"Who told you that you were naked?"

God had not pointed this out to them, He had not made them embarrassed by their own bodies, He had not caused shame upon them, but He asked them where the thought had come from that they were now naked.

That which is meant to shame us, or separate us from God, never comes from God Himself. He would never place us in condemnation, or heap guilt upon us, that is always the work of the devil.

For each of us, when we sin, or do what we know in our hearts is wrong, it is never God who will shame us. Rather, He will come looking for us, continue to journey with us, and ask us the hard questions.

This week, if you are faced with guilt over something you may have done, take it to God and allow Him to walk with you through it, knowing that His love for you is far greater than anything the devil is accusing you of.

Prayer

Lord, I thank you for your unconditional love that goes beyond all I could ever dream or imagine. I thank you that no matter what I do, think, or say, you continue to offer me love, grace and mercy.

God, I am so grateful that you wash me anew every morning, that you never hold my past against me, but you continue to look at me through rose-coloured glasses and you forgive my every sin.

Lord Jesus, I thank you that there is no condemnation in you, no shame, no need to feel embarrassed, for I know that in you I am redeemed and set free.

Thank you, Lord, that I need not fear 'being naked', for you see me as I am, and you choose to love me anyway. You love me regardless of my nakedness before you.

Jesus, teach me to love others the way you love me, help me to be unconditional, to show grace, and to offer mercy.

For you Lord, are the rock on which we stand, the perfect example of what pure love looks like, let me follow in your foot-steps I pray.

Amen

Our Story

Psalm 139:16 (NLT)

You saw me before I was born. Every day of my life was recorded in your book. Every moment was laid out before a single day had passed.

For each of us, God has written our story. He has woven a tale into each of our lives, and filled it with dreams, with hope and with love.

However, within the same story, there is also pain, hurt, disappointment and sadness.

God has not placed those things in our lives, but He uses them for good. He allows them, so that we can be filled with gratitude at how He weaves Himself into the very fabric of all that is wrong and makes it right. He allows our sadness and hurt so that He can shine brighter in filling our lives with joy, peace, and contentment.

There may be days when you wonder if your story is finished, if this could be the end of your journey, if things will always look like this and will never get better. Take heart in knowing that this is never going to be the case. No matter who you are, what age you are, or where you are right now, God can continue to rewrite your story, with a new beginning, a new chapter, and a brand-new start.

Your best days are not behind you, they are yet to come.

We are told in scripture that 'we are a new creation' (2 Corinthians 5:17), this means that the old has passed and something new, and great, and fresh, is about to happen.

God is going to open doors, call you out, and restore the old you into something beautiful.

When you look back over your life, let go of all the disappointments, all the negativity, and all the mistakes, and look forward to all that is yet to come.

God saw your past, but He also sees your future. He sees His creation, the one He loves, and the one that He can and will work through.

Let today be the beginning of the rest of your life, let this be the day a new story is written, the day that hope springs new. Let today be the day that God gives you a fresh start, and out of the rubble He brings forth a ruby.

Prayer

Lord, I thank you that you continue to write my story, that you haven't finished with me yet, but that tomorrow is a new day, one filled with fresh hope.

Lord, help me to always remember that who I was yesterday, or last week, or last year is nowhere near as important as who I am today, and who I will be in the future, thanks to you. You are not interested in the failures of my past, only the successes of my tomorrows.

God, help me to stop judging myself so harshly, but to see myself through your eyes, and to offer myself the grace and mercy that you so freely give me.

Help me to let go of past disappointments, to learn from my mistakes, and to walk with hope into what is yet to come. Remind me of how far I have travelled from who I used to be to who I am now.

Lord God, I thank you that I am stepping into a new chapter, one that is filled with promise for better days, one that is full of opportunities that I couldn't possibly have imagined, yet you always could.

Lord, I thank you for writing my story and shaping it with love. Amen.

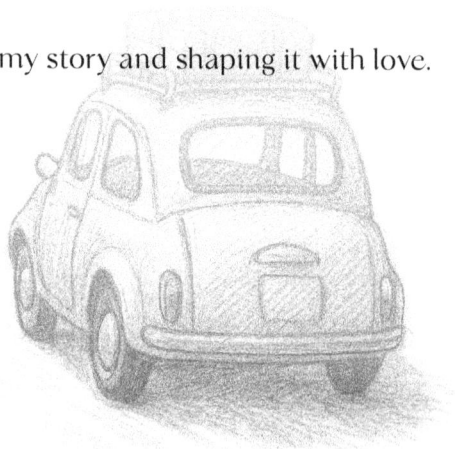

The Truth Sets You Free

John 8:32 (NIV)
Then you shall know the truth, and the truth shall set you free.

The greatest lie that we are told, and that we believe, is that we are not enough.

We are not good enough, we are not clever enough, and we are not pretty enough.

The world is constantly shouting this at us, its all-over social media, it's on our tv and movie screens, it's on billboards, everywhere we look is the lie that we are just never going to be enough. No matter what we do, how we try, how much money or time we spend, we will just never measure up or be enough to compete with everyone else.

The devil knows that if he can get us to believe that we need to be better, we need to try harder or we need to change who we are, then he has a foothold into deceiving us in every other area of our lives.

God wants us to know that we are enough, that regardless of what we look like, what we have achieved, what we are capable of, or what we can or can't do, we are deeply loved by Him.

We are not a series of mishaps or failures, we are not judged by our performance, we are not treasured or valued only by our outward appearance, but the truth is that we are cared for, cherished, and highly valued just as we are.

The thing about lies is that they tie us up in knots, they have us doubting our worth, and they dictate how we feel about ourselves and the situations we find ourselves in. God wants us to live in freedom, He wants us to journey with excitement, He wants us to enjoy the bounty of blessing He has poured out for us, but He knows that if we keep buying in to the lies that the devil is feeding us, we will always live in fear and unbelief.

Today I would encourage you to believe the truth of who God says you are, believe in His great love for you, believe that He created you for good, and believe that above all else, you are enough.

Prayer

Lord, I thank you that you made me in your image, and because of that, I am enough. You created me and chose me; before I was a twinkle in my parents' eyes, you already loved me and had set me apart.

God, help me to know and hold onto the truth of who you say I am, let me not be deceived by all the voices that try to drown out the only voice that matters, your voice God.

Let me hear you above the wind and the waves, above the turmoil in my heart, and above the deception that is playing havoc with my mind.

When I have moments of doubting who I am, of not seeing myself through your eyes, and when I feel disappointed in myself, help me to remember that in you I am a new creation, I am a victor, I am a child of God.

Remind me of the sacrifice of the cross, that Jesus loved me enough to die for me.

Lord, I thank you that not only am I enough, but because of you, I am more than enough.

Amen.

Growth Takes Time

Colossians 1:10 (NLT)
Then the way you live will always honour and please the Lord,
and your lives will produce every kind of good fruit. All the while,
you will grow as you learn to know God better and better.

Many years ago in our garden, we planted what we hoped would one day be big, beautiful, and flourishing, magnolia trees.

Whilst they are beautiful, and produce the loveliest flowers, they certainly could not be described as big. It has taken time for them to get taller and become wider. They certainly haven't grown at the rate I would have liked, and they still don't block the fence like I had imagined they would.

The same could be said for each of us, growth takes time, it is a journey. To be changed mentally, spiritually, or emotionally requires effort, it requires us to do the work, to be willing to have our lives pruned, and our thorns cut back.

We can all agree that growth can be painful, it can be a lot more intense than we expected. But like any good tree, especially fruit trees, for growth to happen and luscious fruit to be produced, there needs to be some cutting back. There needs to be some hacking away at dead branches and prickly thorns.

It's God's greatest desire that we get to know Him better, and that we grow closer to Him. At times that will require us to be planted in new soil, and it may also require that certain things in our lives are pruned and tidied up.

Sometimes the season of growth will seem long winded, it will seem to be taking forever for change to happen, or for circumstances to be different. It may feel that you have been overlooked, or that you've been cast aside, but this is never usually the case. It's just that growth is a journey that takes time and effort.

I would encourage you to look at where you are, where you've come from, and where you're going. Ask God to be with you in your season of growth, and to do all that is needed to bring you closer to Him, that you too may flourish and produce beautiful fruit.

Prayer

Lord, I thank you for the growth in my life, that who I am today is very different to who I was yesterday, last week and last year.

Lord, I know that in some areas of my life growth has been painful, it has come at a cost, and it has hurt. There have been areas that I have tried to withhold from you, but I know you have my best interests at heart. You only prune that which you love, and I know that you love me.

Lord, I pray that you would continue to walk with me as I grow in all the different areas of my life, help me to mature and to flourish, help me to bud and to blossom.

Lord, I am grateful that in you I will not wither, but I will stand tall and become mighty, I will have a good mindset, I will be open to change, I will not be overlooked but I will be amongst those you have called to do great things.

God, I thank you that growth is a necessary part of life, grow me to do great things for you I pray.

Amen.

The Broken-Hearted

Psalm 34:18 (NIV)

God is close to the broken-hearted and saves those who are crushed in spirit.

The pain of heartbreak and of having your spirit crushed can be unbearable. It isn't just an emotional hurt; it can be a very real physical pain. Your body undergoes extreme feelings like that of an actual illness.

These emotions are nothing that can be easily fixed, there's no tablet you can take to make you feel better, no simple words, or quick formula. The only thing that helps is time, and God.

We are promised that God is close to us during our hardest moments, He saves us when we are crushed. He loves on us when we are at our worst, when we feel lost and alone. He journeys with us, holding us when the pain is more than we can bear.

Heartbreak comes in many forms, it can be the actual loss or ending of a relationship, it can be the overwhelming feelings of disappointment, the sadness of plans not going the way we thought they would, or the physical loss of someone we love through death. There is also the heartbreak that comes when a dream dies or is taken away from us, something that we had hoped and planned for, we had looked forward to is gone in a moment, leaving us feeling lost as to what went wrong. But in every instance of heartbreak, God is with us, surrounding us with His love, and pouring His compassion over us. God knows what it is like when things don't go as planned, He has seen His creation completely go astray, He knows the pain involved in the death of a loved one, He saw His son die on a cross. God knows all about heartbreak.

When our spirit is crushed, we feel like there will be no tomorrow, no way we can possibly move forward, no reason to get up in the morning and face the day. But God in His goodness to us, steps in, and saves us. He reminds us of His love for us, His purpose for our lives, and His amazing grace.

Today if you are holding onto the hurt of a broken heart, if you feel crushed, allow God to be your comforter and healer. Give Him your pain, your hurt and your sadness, and allow Him to hold you close.

You are not alone.

Prayer

Father God, I thank you that you know how I feel in every circumstance, especially in heartbreak. You watched as your son was brutally murdered, you know the devastation of loss, the feeling of being crushed.

You see the state of the world today, and you are heartbroken over the way your creation is being decimated, the children you lovingly birthed continue to reject you, and are making a mockery of you.

Lord, in my own heartbreak I thank you that you hold me close, that you see my tears, that you catch them as they fall. Thank you for sending others to love me, to care for me, and to carry me in my time of need. God, you are so good.

Lord, I could not be more grateful for all that you provide for me during this time, you see the state of my heart, my inability to move forward, my struggle with the day to day, and you hold me close, and love me.

Father God, I thank you that because you have suffered, you care for me during my suffering. You know, you understand, and you walk with me through the hard times, and for this, all I can say is thank you.

Amen.

I Will Listen To You

Jeremiah 29:12 (NIV)
Then you will call on me, and come and pray
to me, and I will listen to you'.

What an incredible promise this is to us.

The promise spoken in the words 'I will listen to you'.

God will never be too busy for us, He doesn't pick and choose who He's going to listen to, there's no mention that He may not be interested, or for us to get back to Him some other time. The promise is that if we call on Him, if we come to Him, if we pray to Him, then He will listen.

We have all had times throughout our journey when we have been let down by people, when we thought we could rely on someone only to discover that they don't have time for us or can't come through with what they promised. It's not necessarily done on purpose, but it's just the way life is, people are busy, and situations change.

This is never the case with God. Each one of us is at the centre of His heart. His ear is always attuned to our cry, He is ever watching over us, shining His light in the darkness that surrounds us, and leading us on the path He wants us to travel.

God wants to be in relationship with us, He made a way for us through the death of Jesus on the cross. He allowed His own son to suffer that we might have an open door to Him. That open door allows us to come before Him with all our prayers; our hurts, our needs, and our petitions, and His promise is that in all things He will listen, He will hear, and He will come near to us.

If you need God, He is wholly available to you. He is surrounding you, He is listening to you, He is for you, in all things and through all things. He doesn't make coming to Him complicated or rigorous, He just says to come.

I encourage you to do this today, call out to Him, and come near to Him, and in doing so He will hear you, and lovingly draw you close. For He is the God who listens for your cry, and then encircles you with love.

Prayer

Lord, I call to you now, hear my cry I pray and draw me close.

Father God, you see into my heart and know my needs, you see my tears before they fall, and you know each one of my deepest hurts.

Lord, I thank you that I can come to you without fear or trepidation, that I can lay it all down before you, knowing that there will be no judgement, no discrimination and no rebuff, there will only be love.

I thank you that I am at the centre of your heart, that you are listening to all that I say, and all that I don't. I am so grateful that you hear me, and that words alone need not be spoken for you see me in a way that others never will

God, I pray that you take away the disappointment that I have felt when others have let me down, when they haven't given me the time I've needed, or truly heard me. Help me not to rely on those around me, but to fully rely on you.

Lord, as I step into the unknown and I face hardships, as I call to you in my time of need, and as I walk step by step along the path you lead me, I thank you that I can trust in you, knowing that at all times you will hear my call, and you will listen to the cry of my heart.

Amen.

Humble Beginnings

Where we start in life isn't necessarily where we are going to finish. Your beginnings may have been humble, your birth may have been shrouded in secrecy, and you may have even been told that you weren't planned, but that doesn't exclude you from the plans and purposes that God has for you.

Moses's mother couldn't care for him, they were living in precarious times, where baby boys were being ruthlessly killed, and the only way she could protect her son was to place him in the river and trust that God would care for him.

And this is exactly what God did, He took Moses on a journey that saw him placed in a royal home, and He raised him up to a position of authority. He set him apart and placed within him an incredible faith. The life of Moses may have started out in a less-than-ideal way, but he certainly went on to accomplish incredible things for both God and his people.

Don't let your beginnings determine your ending. Your childhood may not have been great, your upbringing could have been far from perfect, and the family you were raised by may not have seemed like the right fit for you, but God has been with you from the time of your conception through to now.

He has watched over and protected you, He has seen the situations you have had to walk through, and the trials you have faced, and through it all He has held you. You may not have been hidden as a baby in a basket, but you may have endured other life changing moments that have shaped and defined you.

Today believe the truth of who you are, believe that you have been called and set apart, that God in His great love toward you has prepared a hope and a future for you, and that no matter how you may have started out, it is Him who will ensure how you finish.

Prayer

Lord God, I thank you that you are the author of my life, you are the one who determined the day of my birth, and you are the one who orders my steps.

Lord, I thank you for your love, for the way you have watched over and cared for me every day of my life. You have seen each circumstance that I have walked through, you have seen the tears I have cried and the situations I have found myself in, both good and bad. God, I thank you that through it all, you have been there.

My Father, I thank you that you are my constant, the one who stays when everyone else walks away, the one who holds me, who wipes my tears, and who is my ever-present help in times of trouble, you are my all in all.

God, I am grateful that where I started isn't where I'm going to finish. My future is not determined by my past, but each day is a new chapter, a new beginning, one that is orchestrated by you.

Lord, I believe that you have called me, you set me apart, and you have great things in store for me, this is the truth that I will forever hold onto.

Amen.

Gather Together

Matthew 18:20 (NIV)
For where two or three gather in my name, there am I with them.

Jesus wants us to gather, to come together with other believers, to set aside time to meet with those who are of the same faith as us, and when we do, He will be there in the midst.

There is safety in numbers, there is strength, there is encouragement. When we gather, we become a force to be reckoned with. The devil would have us believe that we are better on our own, that we can do life just as well by ourselves, but this is one of his many ploys to keep us isolated. He likes to divide and conquer, He knows that when we gather with other believers there is a supernatural power that comes from on high, that we are no longer operating in our strength but in God's. The devil doesn't want us walking together, being in unity with each other, he would rather keep us apart, that way he can control the narrative, he can continue with his deceptive and manipulative ways.

God created us to live in community, to journey together, to share our lives with others, to be both blessed and a blessing. He wants us to pray for others and have them pray for us. This can only happen when we gather, when we are part of a local church or bible study or women's group. When we gather in His name the atmosphere changes, miracles happen, heaven opens and prayers are heard, for He is in the midst.

Jesus wants to meet with us and to bless us, so He has placed people in our lives who will help us to grow, who will walk with us through the hard days, who will cover us in prayer when we no longer know what to pray ourselves. He places us in circles where we are held and loved, and where in turn we will hold and love others.

God Himself said in Genesis 2:18 'It is not good for man to be alone'. We were never meant to do life on our own, we were meant to be with our people, our tribe, our brothers and sisters in Christ. We are meant to gather 'in His name'.

Today I would encourage you to find your circle, and let Jesus meet you in the midst.

Prayer

Lord Jesus, I thank you for those you have placed in my circle, those who I can pray with and pray for, those who are of the same faith, those who stand with me in the fray.

Lord, I thank you for the opportunity to gather with other believers, other women who are likeminded in their dedication to you, those who honour you, who choose each day to bring glory to you in all they do.

Father God, I pray for my brothers and sisters, that you would arm them with a supernatural strength, that they would know you in a powerful and mighty way, that they would rise up with wings like eagles, that they would be bold in sharing their faith and that they would pray without ceasing.

Lord, I thank you for the opportunities that we have to stand together, to openly worship, to study the bible, to sing, to pray for each other and to love each other.

God, I thank you for each of the saints you have surrounded me with, for the wisdom they carry, the words they have imparted and the joy they have shared, thank you for the blessing of calling them friends.

Amen.

Giftings From God

1 Peter 4:10 (GNT)
Each one, as a good manager of God's different gifts, must use for
the good of others the special gift he has received from God.

Each of us are assigned giftings and talents from God. To some He has given the gift of speaking, others wisdom, prophecy, administration, encouragement, hospitality and so on.

No matter what your gift may be, there is a requirement that you use it to bless others. God didn't bestow talents or gifts on you for you to hide them away, but rather He wants you to share them with the world.

God has given me the ability to write, to share words on paper that would bless and encourage others. So, in being faithful to Him, I share thoughts, poems, devotions and stories in order that I might bring hope to others, and in doing so, glorify God.

Writing for me is not about getting my name in print, it's not about fame or fortune, but rather, it's all about God, who He is, and the blessing He has poured out in my life. This is what I love to write about.

Whatever each of us do, our main aim should always be about honouring God, about acknowledging all that He has given us, and by giving back. No matter where we are on our journey of life, we need to open our hands and share what we have with others.

We would have nothing if He hadn't given it to us in the first place. His gifts are what we are fortunate enough to call our talents.

If you are blessed with the ability to cook hearty meals, then share those meals with others. If God has given you a beautiful home, then open the doors to invite others in. If you have great administration skills, then put those skills to use in your church or community. If God has given you the gift of speaking or preaching, then give it your all by sharing the love of Jesus with others.

Regardless of where your gifts or talents lie, ask God to use you, ask Him to lead you where He wants you to be, that you might be a blessing to others.

Prayer

Father God, I thank you for all the blessings you have given me, for my home, my family and friends, the food on my table, and the many provisions that I have often taken for granted.

Lord, I also thank you for the gifts and talents that you have bestowed upon me, for the abilities I have to do things for you and for others. Thank you, Lord, that I can do things that I see as fun and enjoyable, yet those same things are often seen as a great blessing to those around me.

God, help me to be more aware of those who are in need, those who could do with a friend, a warm meal, or a word of encouragement. Lead me to those who need a helping hand, those who need a shoulder to cry on, or a place to feel safe.

Lord, help me to share from all that I have, remembering that everything I have is a gift from you. Let me give back in word, in deed, and in action. Let your gift to me, be my gift to others.

God, I pray, may I always use my talents for your glory, honouring you in all that I do.

Amen.

Come To Jesus

Matthew 11:28 (NIV)
Come to me all you who are weary and burdened, and I will give you rest.

We are called to come to God as we are, with all our burdens, our weaknesses, our disappointments, and our hurts. Nowhere in the bible does it say that we should come when we have our lives sorted out, when our ducks are all lined up in a row, or when we are free from problems or issues, but rather we should come when we are weary, when we are heavy-laden, and it is then that He will give us rest.

So often we get caught up in the belief that our lives need to be perfect, that we need to have everything all together, that God couldn't possibly accept us in our soiled state, so we therefore need to get ourselves sorted out so that we can be found to be of value in His eyes.

If this was the truth, what was the point of Jesus dying? He didn't die for a perfect and well put together world, but rather He died for the lost, for the weak, for the needy, and for the broken. Jesus calls us to come to Him as we are, no matter where we are on our journey, if we are lost in sin, if we are knee deep in depression, if we are trudging through the trenches, or walking through the drought of the desert. No matter how bad the state of our hearts or our lives, He still calls us back to Him. The road we are travelling, and the journey we are on, all lead to the same destination, and that is the feet of Jesus. We just need to keep putting one foot in front of the other until we find ourselves face to face with Him.

The church is not a place filled with perfect people, but rather it is a place where people serve a perfect God. It is because of the love of God that we are called into relationship, it is not because of anything we may have done, but it is all because of His great love for us.

I would remind you today that no matter how you look, how you feel, or how you have behaved, God wants you to come to Him, just as you are.

Prayer

Father God, I thank you that I can come to you just as I am. I am so grateful that I don't have to play games, I don't have to impress you, or try to be someone I'm not, but all I have to do is come.

Lord, I hand you my heart, I give over to you every part of me, and I ask that you have your way, and that you fulfill your purpose within me. Use me for your glory, that in turn I would bring honour back to you.

Lord, help me to let go of my burdens, to hand over my worries and concerns, and trust that you have it all in control. I know that anxiety changes nothing, but that you can change everything, help me to remember that when I'm holding tightly to the burdens of my heart.

I thank you for your perfect peace, for the rest and refreshing that only you can give, and I ask that you help my weary soul to find it's hope in you.

As you walk beside me, step by step, I thank you Jesus, that you are the keeper of my heart.

Amen.

The Lord Directs Our Steps

Proverbs 16:9 (AMP)
A man's mind plans his way [as he journeys through life],
But the Lord directs his steps and establishes them.

Every day we face choices, and we make decisions.

We have endless possibilities of all that we can do, as our lives are full of long hallways and open doors.

There are so many incredible options available to us, and sometimes this can be overwhelming, especially when trying to decide which is the best way to go.

Thankfully, as Christians, we have a God who goes before us, who knows the beginning from the end, who can see the good, the bad and the ugly.

We are blessed that we are loved by someone who wants only great things for us, who wants us to journey on the path that leads to happiness, to wholeness and to the place of victory.

In knowing all of this, why is it that we sometimes choose to make plans without the involvement of God? Why do we say yes to things then ask God later if it was a good idea?

Surely it would be better to pray first rather than regret later.

God doesn't want to withhold good from us, He doesn't want us to miss out, or to be left behind, but neither does He want us to jump in the deep end and then realise that maybe this is the place we could drown.

God wants us to share our hopes, our dreams, and our plans with Him. He wants us to desire His blessing for that which we seek. He wants to be fully involved in our lives, not just called on when things fall to pieces or go pear-shaped.

Today, invite God into the planning process, share the vision with Him, and allow Him to make the final decision, knowing that He has your back in all things, and that His ways are always best.

Prayer

Lord, I thank you that you are the one who directs my steps, the one who leads me and shows me the way to go, the one who opens and closes doors and establishes my plans.

God, help me to always remember that I need you, that I can't do life on my own, no matter how much I think I can. Help me to know that in all things I need to fully rely on you.

Help me to pray first rather than regret later, to bring everything before you, to have open and honest discussions with you, holding nothing back, but sharing my deepest thoughts and feelings with my greatest love.

God, I thank you that your desire is to bless me, to shower me with your love, and to lead me to places where my faith will grow, and my life will flourish. Lord help to trust that you know best, and to follow you even when I can't see what's ahead.

Lord Jesus, in you I place my trust, as I know that you are the only way.

Amen.

Who Is God To You?

Matthew 16:15-16 (MSG)
He pressed them "How about you? Who do you say I am?"
Simon Peter said, "You're the Christ, the
Messiah, the Son of the Living God."

I f God were to ask you who you thought He was, what would you say? Is He just a faraway being that you don't really know? Is He the main player in a fairy-tale you heard about in your younger years? Or would you answer the same as Peter did? Would you say that he is the Messiah, the Almighty Christ, and your personal Saviour?

For each of us the entity of God can mean so many varied things, and He can represent something different for us all.

For many, we may see God as someone who watches over us, however not in a loving way, but rather as someone ready to judge and punish us for all that we have done wrong. Others see Him as someone to blame for the atrocities that take place in the world, and there are those who see Him as a crutch when life becomes too hard to deal with on our own. But for those of us who call ourselves Christians, we see Him as a loving and just God, who is with us in and through all things, who walks beside us and behind us, leading us, loving us, and saving us on our journey through life.

Each of us must decide for ourselves who God is, this isn't something that others can do for us, we can't claim the faith of our family, for we need to have our own experience. We need to decide if God is our Saviour, or if He is just a far off, seldom thought of being, that has no real place in our world. The decision we make will have long lasting effects on our future, it will determine how we look at life, where we place our hope, and whether we choose to have faith in anyone other than ourselves. Who God is, is truly one of the biggest questions in life.

Today I would encourage you to seek for yourselves who God is, and I pray that you would find Him to be the Way, the Truth and the Life.

Prayer

Lord, I thank you that I can stand secure in the knowledge of who you are, I can rest in peace knowing that you are my Saviour.

God, I am more than grateful that you have shown yourself to me in so many ways, that you have made your presence known and that I can feel your Holy Spirit.

Father, you are my healer, my friend, my confidant, my rock and my high place. I am safe with you. There is nowhere that I journey that you don't go with me.

Lord, place my feet on higher ground that I might shout your name and bring glory to you in all things. Let my voice of praise be louder than all that would try to drown me out, let me sing of your goodness and worship you as the only true God.

May I always stand firm in your truth and walk only in your ways.

Amen.

Love Your Neighbour

We have often heard it said that we need to love our neighbour as ourselves, but who is our neighbour?

Is it literally the person we live next door to? Or the person we share a fence line with? Is it the person we chat to when we come out our backdoor? Or the one we argue with over barking dogs, rowdy teenagers, overhanging trees, or late-night parties?

Our neighbour may not just be those living on either side of our homes, but it can be our work colleagues, our sporting team mates, our church community, our school friends, and our relatives.

Our neighbours are anyone and everyone. They are those we see each day, those we journey through life with, those with different ideas than ours, and those who may rub us up the wrong way.

Jesus wants us to love all of those around us as much as we love ourselves. He wants us to go the extra mile for them, to be available to help them out during hard times. He wants us to rejoice and celebrate with them, but also to support and encourage them.

There are many that we would and could happily do this for, but there are also just as many we would rather avoid, or sidestep, rather than go out of our way for them. We don't want to love them, we don't want to put ourselves out for them, and we don't want to share the fruits of our labour with them.

Yet, as disciples and followers of Jesus, we want to do what we have been called to do. We want to love in the way that He has taught us, we want to show His grace and kindness to others, and that includes our neighbours, whoever they may be.

Today, I would encourage you to share the love, to turn the other cheek, to put off self, and to allow Jesus to shine through you.

Let today be the day that you love your neighbour as yourself.

Prayer

Lord God, I thank you for the reminder that we are called to love others as you have loved us. That regardless of how we may feel, we are to show our neighbour mercy, grace and kindness.

Lord, help me to love my neighbour, be that the person next door, my less than loveable colleague, my sporting opponent, or that one person I can barely tolerate, help me to love like you do.

God, I pray that you would give me a heart that is filled with compassion, that cares for others more than myself, that I would be willing to go the extra mile without expecting anything in return. Help me to support and encourage those who hurt, those who need to see you in action, those who have been trampled by life.

Father, let me be a vessel of your love, a blessing to those around me, a light in the darkness. Let my neighbour see you in all that I do, this is my prayer today.

Amen.

Make Time To Pray

Mark 1:35 (NLT)
Before daybreak the next morning, Jesus got up
and went out to an isolated place to pray.

Jesus set aside time to pray, He took Himself away from the crowds, the family members, the friends, and He went off by Himself and spent time with God.

What does your early morning ritual look like? Do you set aside time in the morning to read your bible, to pray, to hear from God?

It's not always easy getting up early, it can be a sacrifice, but it's in doing this that you give God your best.

The time you spend with Him in the morning is what can set you up for the day. It's the time to pour out all your burdens, your desires and your needs. It's also the time to hear from God, to ask what He would require of you, to seek His plan and His purpose for your life.

Jesus went to an isolated place to pray, He needed space away from those who were surrounding Him, He needed the quietness to connect with His Father, and to seek His will. When Simon went to look for

Jesus, he told Him that everyone was wondering where He was, and Jesus responded that He needed to go somewhere to preach, as that is why He had come.

When Jesus had spent time with His Father, His purpose was reignited. He knew what He was there for and what He needed to do. Jesus needed to fulfil the will of the Father, and to do what He had been sent to do.

This is what happens when we set time aside to be with God, when we have a daily ritual of being in prayer and reading His word. It is when we invite Him on our journey, and we make Him a priority, we are then reminded of our purpose, it prepares our hearts for our calling.

I would encourage you today to spend your mornings with God, not just asking from Him, but listening to Him and hearing from Him, this is the best way to prepare you for the day ahead.

Prayer

Lord Jesus, I thank you for the time I can spend with you, the time that is precious and irreplaceable. God, I thank you for your presence in my life, for the impact that it has on my day to day, in every area of my being.

Thank you, God, that when I spend my mornings with you it prepares me for all that lies ahead, it sets me up, it gives me peace and strength and hope. Because of the time I set aside, you saturate my soul with your Spirit and fill me to overflowing.

Lord, I pray that you go with me through this day, that you watch over me, that you help me to remain still in the face of that which would make me anxious, help me to keep my eyes fixed on you when the world tries to call me away.

Jesus, I pray that your Holy Spirit would guide me and lead me, that your presence would stay with me, and that in all things, I would remain held by you.

Amen.

Let Them Carry You

The people you surround yourself with are far more important than you think, they can be the making or breaking of you. They can be the very ones who lead you to the feet of Jesus or carry you to Him when you can't get there yourself.

This incredible story in Luke is only very short, but it certainly sends a message about the friends that this man, a paraplegic, kept. When they knew that Jesus was in town, and that He was healing people, they grabbed their friend and did all they could to bring Him to the Healer. When they couldn't get into the house through the front door, due to the crowds, they went the extra mile and climbed up on the roof to lower him down into the middle of where Jesus sat.

What a journey the man experienced that day. He knew that Jesus could heal him, but he had no way of getting to Him, however, his friends did. His heart must have been soaring as he was carried through the crowds, with lots of pushing and shoving, trying to get to where the healing was taking place. Once there, he would have been overcome with disappointment to not be able to get in, only to be buoyed up once again when his friends came up with a new plan of lowering him through the roof. What an amazing story, and yet it doesn't end there, Jesus in that moment forgives his sins and heals him. The faith of this man and his friends changed the entire trajectory of his life.

There are times when we can't fight for ourselves, when we can't move forward, and when our faith alone is small in comparison to our need. It is at these times when we need others. We need strong men and women of God surrounding us, lifting us in prayer, holding our hands up when our strength is weak, and bringing us to Jesus.

Today I would encourage you to find your tribe, those who will go the extra mile for you when the going gets tough, those who won't give up, and those who will journey to great heights to get you to where you need to be. Remember too, you need to be this person for someone else, for someone who can't keep fighting, who has reached the end, and needs their mat carried, be that friend today.

Prayer

Lord, thank you for the timely reminder about those I allow in my circle, and those I spend time with. I thank you God for the beautiful and faithful friends you have placed in my life, those who encourage me, strengthen me, and bring me closer to you.

Help me to always be the one who goes the extra mile, who sees the open doors of opportunity and looks for ways to walk through it. Lord, help me to not be consumed by purely my own interests, but for the interests of those in my circle, that I might find ways to bring them closer to you.

Father God, I know a journey is best taken with others, so I ask that you continue to place the right people around me, people who would challenge my behaviour and attitudes, who would stretch me in my faith, and who would ultimately walk with me towards you.

Lord, may I be humble enough to allow my mat to be carried, and may I always be willing to carry the mat for others. I ask that my heart would be receptive to wherever I find myself, and that I would never be too proud to come to you by whatever means is necessary.

I thank you for your forgiveness of my sins, and the healing of my body.

Amen

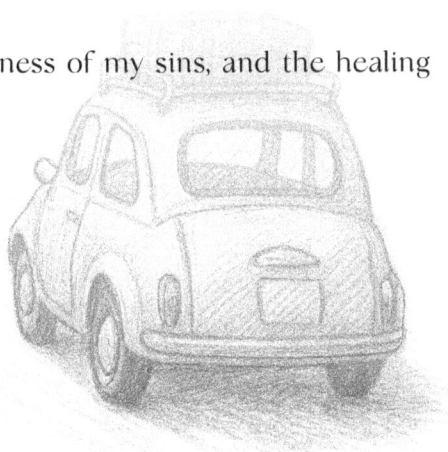

His Hand Of Blessing

Psalm 139:5 (NLT)
You go before me and follow me. You place
your hand of blessing on my head.

There are days when life can be totally overwhelming. Where we feel like there is so much going on that we can't possibly cope with one more thing. Days where we feel like the battle we fight is too big, and that we are doing it alone. We feel flattened, worn down, and empty.

Yet, in the depths of our heart, we know with absolute certainty, that although we 'feel' alone, we never are.

Our God, the creator of the universe, the all-powerful one, is with us in every circumstance. He surrounds us on all sides and walks into battle with us. He stands beside us as we face the impossible, and He goes before us to ensure our way. Every step of our journey, our God is there.

Our days may feel empty, but with God we can be sure that our hearts will always be full. If we stay close to Him, giving Him the time and space to whisper to us, to lead us, and to carry us, then we will never be alone, for He is our constant.

From the early morning sunrise, until the sun sets again at night, God is with us. He blesses us in every season of our lives. Just because we don't always feel His touch, it doesn't mean that He isn't working. He is in the background, preparing the way, opening the doors, and moving in the heavenlies in order that we might walk forward.

If you can't see the answer, if you don't have the go ahead, or if you still seem to be waiting, keep trusting God. He hasn't forgotten you or walked off and left you. He is still with you, He still has a plan, and He is still on your side.

Keep your hope in Him today, knowing that in all things, He is with you, and His hand of blessing is on you.

Prayer

Lord Jesus, I thank you that you are with me today, tomorrow and always. I know that you hold my hand and lead me by still waters, that no matter where I may find myself in life, you too are there.

God, my heart rests in the knowledge that I am never alone, that your presence surrounds me and keeps me in peace, that no matter what circumstance I might find myself in, you are with me, and you are blessing me.

Whether I go into battle, or fall prey to anxiety and distress, I know that I am under the cover of your wings, that you will provide and protect, and that your love is my safe place.

As I rise each morning help me to remain focused on you, to spend time in your presence and to gird my loins with your truth. Help me not to waver in all that I know, but to hold onto your promises and stand firm in you.

And Lord as I lie down each night, let me sleep in peace, for you are the God who watches over me, who holds me, and who loves me through all things.

Amen.

Why God Says No

Genesis 2:16-17 (MSG)
*God commanded the man "You can eat from any tree in the
garden, except from the tree of knowledge of good and evil.
Don't eat from it, the moment you eat from it, you're dead."*

God had given Adam and Eve the most beautiful environment to
live in. They had the lifestyle that most of us can only dream
of; surrounded by incredible beauty, with nothing more to do
in life but enjoy each other, their home, and their time with God. They
had only been given one restriction, not to eat from a certain tree in the
garden, and yet that one thing, that small instruction from God, was
what tripped them up and became their downfall.

For each of us there are no-go zones, and do not enter signs, there
are journeys that we should never venture on. For our own good, God
has doors that He wants kept closed. He has places He wants us to avoid,
and He has things He wants kept untouched. Not because He wants us
to go without, but because He wants us to be safe.

Once Adam and Eve were deceived into believing that there was no harm in eating from the one tree that they were told not to touch, everything changed. Although the death they experienced was not literal, the life that they knew certainly died. They now hid their bodies in shame, they hid from God in fear, and their once easy-going life was exchanged for hard manual labour.

God gives us instructions for a reason, they are not to hurt us or control us, but they are to keep us safe, to keep us free from problems, and to keep us close to Him.

There's nothing the deceiver wants more than to trick you into believing that it's ok to do that one small thing, that's it's not a big deal, that God really won't care. Don't believe those lies.

God has called you and set you apart for a purpose. If He has asked you not to do something, if He has put up a 'do not enter' sign, then it's for your benefit. Walk with Him, stay attuned to what He has to say, and don't believe any of the lies of the enemy.

Know the truth and let it set you free.

Prayer

Lord, I thank you that you have my best interests at heart, that all you do and say is for my benefit and my good. Help me to always remember that, in every circumstance.

God, I pray that you keep me close to you, help me to stay attuned to your Holy Spirit, hearing your whisper above every other noise. Let your voice be the one that I hear the loudest, when there are so many others clamouring for my attention.

Lord, give me the wisdom and understanding to know when to go and when to stay, when to walk through doors, and when to trust that they are closed for a reason. Help me to see the bigger picture and not become overwhelmed by my own desires, wants and needs.

Father God, let me accept that you say no for a reason, that you see the beginning from the end, and that you are the one who is ultimately in control, may I always be willing to release all that I think I can control to you.

God, search me and know me, grant me a teachable and pliable spirit so that all I do brings glory to you.

Amen.

Jesus Sees You

Luke 10:40 (NIV)

But Martha was distracted by all the preparations that had to be made. She came to Him and asked, "Lord, don't you care that my sister has left me to do the work by myself? Tell her to help me."

For each of us there is a deep core need to feel cared for, to feel loved, and to know that we are valued. We want to know that our thoughts and feelings matter, it is our hope that Jesus sees our tears, our disappointments, our hurts, and our fears, and that He cares about what we are struggling through.

Martha was no different than the rest of us, she had the same basic needs as we do, she wanted to be seen by Jesus. However, in her desire to serve Him, she became so wrapped up in doing, that she forgot to just be. She was so busy and distracted, that she missed the opportunity to spend time with Jesus, just basking in His presence.

It was during this time, when she was overwhelmed by all she had to do, that she became bitter towards her sister. She saw Mary just sitting at the feet of Jesus, not doing anything to help her, not serving, not assisting, but rather just being with Him, and she was completely distraught.

It is here we see her cry out to Jesus, 'Lord don't you care......?'

We have all been there, we have cried out to God, we have petitioned Him, fallen at His feet, and in our distress, we have uttered the very same words, 'Don't you care?'

And then Martha goes one step further and advises Jesus as to what He should do next, she says 'Tell her to help me.'

I think there is a bit of Martha in all of us. I know that I have found myself crying out to God with options on ways He could change a situation or move in my life. I have presumed that He may need my help on the journey I am walking, and so in my sorrowful prayers I have given Him suggestions on what He might like to do for me.

However, I have learnt, often the hard way, that Jesus knows better than I do, that He has a better way, and that I need to just trust Him with the outcome for each situation.

Today, know that Jesus sees and hears you, let go of the worry and the stress and just be in the moment, be present in His presence.

Prayer

Lord Jesus, I thank you that you see me, that I don't have to struggle or strive, I don't have to work harder or prove myself, but you see me just as I am.

Lord, help me to remember that you want me to be present with you, to set aside time to spend with you in the stillness, no rushing, no overthinking, no serving, but just being with you.

Lord, help me to focus on what is important, knowing that my relationship with you is not about what I do for you, but rather it is about the state of my heart towards you, and towards others.

Remind me that there is nothing greater than sitting at your feet, than spending time in prayer with you, listening for your small still voice.

Help me to remember that you don't need my advice, you managed to create the entire world without me, so why would you need my help now. Lord, give me the ability to trust you and to lean on you, and not on my own understanding.

Lord, I thank you that you see me, just as I am, and that you love me. Thank you that I can come to you, sit at your feet, and know that I am welcomed into your presence. May I never take this blessing for granted.

Amen.

Give Thanks

1 Thessalonians 5:18 (NIV)
Give thanks in all circumstances, for this is
God's will for you in Christ Jesus.

There are days when giving thanks comes easy, and then there are all those other days.

The days when nothing goes right, when relationships break down, when fear takes over, and when disaster strikes. It's on those days that we struggle to see the good, to remain grateful, and to remember to give thanks to God in all circumstances, regardless of what that may costs us.

It is on these days that we need to dig a little deeper, when we realise that we are giving thanks because of who God is, not because of what we may be going through. We are thanking Him for His faithfulness, His love towards us, and His protection over us.

There are many examples in the bible of Godly people who suffered through difficult times, yet they remained grateful towards God, not withholding praise from Him, but in sacrifice they offered up to Him all that they were and all that they had.

Job was an incredible example of this, he had lost everything, his whole family was wiped out, yet during his heartbreak, he continued to worship God, he continued to remain steadfast in his dedication to God, realising that he wasn't entitled to anything, but all that he had was a gift from God, and for this he was grateful.

King David is another amazing example of a man showing thankfulness during times of despair. We know from reading the book of Psalms that the journey of David's life was one epic story after another. He went from mountain tops to valleys more often than most people we know, but throughout his life, he continued to thank God for all that He was doing, and all that He would do. He never doubted that God would show up for Him, and he continually proclaimed the goodness of God.

Nowhere in the bible does it tell us to only praise God on the good days, to be grateful only in the moments when things are going well. Rather, we are instructed to always praise God, in all things and through all things.

Today I would encourage you, no matter how tough things may be, remember the truth of who God is, thank Him for His faithfulness, and praise Him in all circumstances.

Prayer

Lord Jesus, I thank you that you are my constant, my shelter in the storm, my rock and the fortress that I can run to.

Lord, forgive me for the all the times that I have been neglectful in thanking you, in showing you honour, and in giving you praise. I know that without you I wouldn't be where I am today, and my journey would look very different without your leading.

God, on the days when I feel overwhelmed, when I'm tired, and when I simply don't have the words to offer up to you, remind me to dig a little deeper. Remind me that pouring out my praise and thanksgiving is the lifeline that will in turn give me the strength I need to keep going.

Heavenly Father, I thank you for who you are, not what you do. You are the Alpha and Omega, the biggest and the best. You have placed the stars in the sky, and you know them by name. You created all things, including me, and I am forever grateful that you choose to call me your own.

God, help me to remember that even on my hard days I can praise you, in every circumstance, good and bad, you alone are worthy.

Thank you, Jesus, for all you are.

Amen.

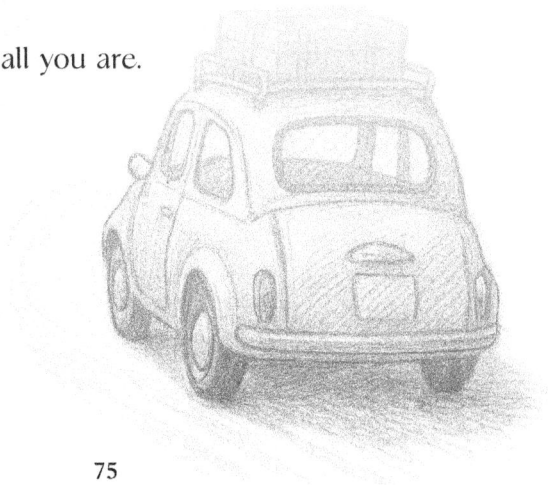

Stop Doubting And Believe

John 20:27 (NIV)
Then he said to Thomas, "Put your finger here; see my hands. Reach
out your hand and put it into my side. Stop doubting and believe."

Within the heart of each of us lives a Thomas. A doubter, a nay-sayer, a non-believer. The one who needs to see to believe, who needs proof, and who requires an earthly answer to every spiritual question.

Thomas wasn't with the other believers when Jesus appeared to them, he wasn't part of the celebrations, the unexpected joy, or the unbelievable miracle. He didn't get to be in the room when Jesus first reappeared, so he's feeling left out, he's totally out of the loop, and he's at a complete loss as to how to fathom what exactly has happened.

There are times when we all doubt just as Thomas did, when we can't possibly believe something that just seems too far-fetched, or too good to be true. We want to have hope, we want to trust in the miracle, and we most certainly want to believe in the promises of God, but it's never quite that simple.

Jesus understood where Thomas was coming from, He could see through to his heart, He could read the mixed emotions that were running through his mind, and He could certainly see the doubt on Thomas's face. Yet, He never ridiculed him, He never put him down, and He certainly never cast Thomas aside. Jesus, in His kindness, offered Thomas exactly what he needed, physical proof. He gave Thomas the opportunity to reach out and touch Him, to see and feel where the nails had been. He allowed Thomas grace on His journey to belief, He didn't push, He simply provided the truth.

Jesus offers this same grace to each of us, He understands our inability to believe what we can't see, and although His greatest desire is that we would not doubt, but have childlike faith, He still chooses to meet us exactly where we are.

Today hand over your doubts, and your unbelief and let Jesus draw you to Him, that you may find yourself in a place of knowing exactly who He is, and who you are in Him.

Prayer

Lord God, I thank you that you still love me even when I doubt, even during my moments of unbelief, when I grapple with trusting in the unknown, in what I can't see.

Lord, I thank you that you see my heart, you understand my struggles and you work with me as I come to you with child-like faith.

Father God, in so many ways I am like Thomas, I want to believe, I want to trust, I want what the others have, yet I find myself needing proof, needing to see and feel and touch to know for sure.

Lord, forgive me for my doubt, for the times I still search for reassurance and answers, when I know in my heart that all I need to do is put my trust in you.

God, I ask that you lead me into the quiet assurance of belief, of hope, of the knowledge that all that you say is true. Guide me as I follow you, and teach me to rely not on myself, but wholly upon you. Lord this is my prayer.

Amen.

Learn What Pleases Him

Ephesians 5:10 (TLB)
Learn as you go along what pleases the Lord.

Within the heart of each of us is the desire to do the things that please God, the things that bring pleasure to Him, and the things that we know will bring us closer to Him.

The Bible gives us great advice on all that we need to do to live a life that pleases God, some of these things come easily and naturally to us, however, there are other things that we all struggle with.

We are to forgive others, even when it's hard, or when we would rather hold a grudge.

We are to walk humbly, not being arrogant or prideful, not exalting ourselves in a place of privilege above others.

We are to speak truth, even when embellishing a story makes it sound more fun, or when not telling the truth can protect us from judgement.

We are to keep our lips free from gossip, not bringing others under the scrutiny of those who would choose to wound them.

We are to work diligently, whether we are being watched or not, remembering that whatever we do, we are doing it for God.

We are to be generous, sharing all that we have with those less fortunate than ourselves, not hoarding our possessions, but giving from our abundance.

We are to care for the widows and the orphans, for the elderly and the weak, helping them in their time of need, protecting them, and offering them a place in our own families.

We are to have a teachable spirit, not thinking that we are all knowing, remembering that only God knows all.

We are to be the hands and feet of Jesus, going on whatever journey He calls us, and reaching out in love to those He brings across our path.

We are to offer grace and restoration to all those around us, remembering that Jesus came to bring life to all.

In everything that we do, in all that we are, may we always live a life that is pleasing to God.

Prayer

Lord, my greatest desire is also my greatest struggle, and that is to live a life that is pleasing to you. To put you first in all things, to make you Lord overall.

God, I pray that you help me as I set my heart on you, as I determine to live a Christ centred life, one where you are my focus and where everything else fades away.

Lord, help me to take my eyes off myself, and place them where they should be, on you. Help me to look outward and not inward, to be more interested in others, to care for them and love them the way you do. Help me to be humble, thinking more highly of those around me than I do of myself.

God, change my attitude so that I am more in tune with your Spirit, let me be led by you so that I don't get carried away by my own thoughts, feelings and emotions. Ground me in your ways that I might follow you, always and forever.

Amen.

We Are His Greatest Creation

PSALM 50:10 (NIV)

For every animal of the forest is mine, and the cattle on a thousand hills.

Everything on the earth was created by God, and everything on the earth belongs to God. There is nothing that we can add to what He has made.

There is absolutely nothing that we can give Him that He doesn't already have, there is no gift, no sacrifice, no burnt offerings. There is only thing that He requires from us, and that is that we would bring ourselves to Him in full surrender.

Our lives are more important to God than all the birds in the air, the fish in the sea, and all that lives on the land. We are His greatest creation, and what brings Him the most joy.

He takes pleasure in hearing our praise toward Him and seeing our lives flourish.

It is His desire that we spend time with Him, sharing our hopes, our dreams, our disappointments, and our failings. He wants to intimately be involved in every part of our lives, that regardless of where we are on our journey, He wants us to turn to Him in every situation and make Him our first and our last. This is the greatest gift that we can offer, that we would take the life that He has given us, and we would freely give it back, that we would honour Him with our dedication towards Him.

God gives each of us free will, He doesn't force us to do anything that we don't want to do, He doesn't insist we follow His ways or walk on His chosen path. He simply holds out His hand and calls us to Him. What we do with that calling is completely up to us. He loves us enough to let us make our own choices, and therefore He never enforces His desires onto us.

Today, as you think on all that God has created and all that He owns, think also on all that He freely gives. He has given you the life that you are living, He has given you free will, He has given you hope and blessing, and most importantly He has given you His great love.

Enjoy the blessings of God today.

Prayer

Father God, I thank you for the gift of life, for all you have created, and for the breath that you have breathed into me.

I thank you that of all the incredible things you created, the mountains, the oceans, and the vast array of animals, that you would choose us, mere men and women, to be your friends.

I am so grateful that before the beginning of time you placed my name into the book of life. You had purposed a plan for me, one that included peace and prosperity, a life that included us walking together through the good and the bad.

Thank you, God, for your sacrifice, that because of your love for me, you willingly allowed your only Son to die to take my place. You allowed your heart to be broken in order that mine would be healed. I can never offer enough praise for what you have done.

Lord, I am in awe that you find great joy in me, that you see me in a way that the world never will, that you long for me to spend time with you, soaking in your presence.

God, I pray that in all I do, you would be glorified, that my life would be honouring to you, and that I would bring you praise.

Amen.

What Is In Your Hand?

Exodus 4:2 (NIV)
Then the Lord said to him, "What is that in your hand?"
"A staff," he replied.

There are times in each of our lives when we question God about what He wants us to do. What His plan is for our future, whether we should pursue a ministry, or what career path He would like us to embark on.

We agonise over decisions and desperately long to hear His voice, especially in an audible way, telling us which direction to take or what would be the best course of action.

We are not alone in our calling out to God, Moses too needed to hear from Him, and He asked God for a sign. God used the staff that Moses was holding, the meaningless object that was used to keep sheep in line, this is what God chose to become an instrument of miracles.

God takes what we are holding in our hands, and He does something beautiful with it. He doesn't need big fanfare situations, He doesn't need us to appear worthy in the eyes of the world, He doesn't require us to hold degrees or doctorates, all He wants is for us to be willing and useable.

You may feel that you have nothing to offer, but God sees it very differently. He sees you as an open door of possibility in fulfilling His plans and purposes, both for you and through you.

If you can sing, if you can write, if you can teach, or if you are hospitable and can open your home, do it for the glory of God. No matter what your gifts or talents, when you hold them loosely in your hands and allow Him to use them, something incredible will take place.

There is nothing more beautiful than being a vessel that the Lord can use, being open to opportunities and being available to Him. There is nothing more powerful than letting Him take what you have in your hands and allowing Him to make something from it.

As you journey through the ups and downs of life, He will seek you out and enquire of you as to how willing you are to do something for Him, big or small. No matter who you are, or what you do or don't have, God can still use you.

Today I would encourage you to pry open your fingers and give back to God all that He gave to you. Let Him use all that you are to become all that He wants.

Prayer

Father God, I give you all that I am, I hand over all my talents, my giftings, my abilities, and I ask that you use them in whatever way you see fit.

Lord, I know that everything I have in life is from you, that you chose to bestow upon me blessings that far outnumber anything I could ever hope or dream. All that I have is a gift that you have freely given.

I pray now that you would show me how to use what I have, to not only honour you, but to bless those around me. Help me to be willing to share all that I have, to give without expecting anything in return.

Let my voice bring words of peace, let me speak with power and passion, give me opportunity to speak for those who can't speak for themselves, to stand up for those who have been downtrodden.

May my home be an open door, a place that welcomes others, and brings refreshment. Help me not hold too tightly to all I have but let me be willing to bring others in and show them your great love.

God, today I offer back to you all that I am, and all that I have, and I pray that you would use all things for your glory.

Amen.

The Boy With A Dream

The story of Joseph is one that is well known and has been passed down through many generations. The story of a boy who was highly favoured by his father, yet despised by his brothers, the same boy, however, was chosen by God.

The journey of Joseph from the time he was sold by his brothers, until the day he was reunited with them and his father once again, lasted twenty-two years. That is a long time to hold onto a dream and a promise. It is a long time waiting for God to come through, waiting for everything to come to fruition that you had been hoping and praying for.

During that season of waiting Joseph underwent terrible hardship, and spent 13 years in prison, for a crime he never committed. He was falsely accused, he was disappointed, he was overlooked, and he was downcast. Yet, throughout all of this, he continued to cling to God.

We don't always get what we want, or what we think we deserve. Sometimes others will betray us, even those we love. God may whisper promises to us, but sometimes they can be a long time in coming, and we can find it very hard to keep holding on when all seems lost. It's not always easy to stay faithful when we have been hurt, or abandoned, or set against. We can often want revenge or cry out for retribution for all that has been done to us. Sometimes the ugly side of life finds its way to our door, and it's hard.

But if we can learn anything from Joseph, lets learn what it looks like to wait with the right attitude, with a clean heart, and with a forgiving spirit. He never sought to destroy others, and he certainly could have, but rather he chose to hear from God and to follow in His ways.

Joseph is a beautiful example of what it looks like to know God is with you in the valley, but to trust that He will bring you out the other side. To know that no matter how long the wait, it will be worth it in the end, and to be sure that it will be God who has the final say in where your journey begins and ends.

Prayer

Lord, I thank you that my story is being written by you, that on every page there is a plan and a purpose, even when I don't see it.

Lord, as I think on the story of Joseph, I pray that you give me a heart like his, one that is pure, that doesn't seek revenge, that doesn't harbour bitterness, and that stays soft toward you.

Even when all I hope for doesn't come to pass, when the dreams you planted in my heart seem lost, and the prayers I have prayed seem to have fallen on deaf ears, Lord, through all of this, help me to remain faithful to you.

God, help me to trust you in the unknown, when I can't fathom what tomorrow will look like, and I am overwhelmed by today. Help me to hold on when it would be so easy to let go.

Lord, when I am overlooked, when I have been betrayed, when I feel forgotten, remind me that you see all. There is nothing that escapes you, and I know that no matter how many are against me, you are always for me.

Amen

Where Is Your Trust?

Psalm 118:8 (TLB)
It is better to trust the Lord than to put confidence in men.

There are days when trusting in God is easier said than done. It's hard to trust in the unknown when we are barely holding on, when we hit desperate times, and when there appears to be no end in sight to the hardship we are facing.

Sometimes it's hard to fully believe that God has your best interests at heart, that He is working all things together for your good, or that He goes before you into the chasm that is overwhelming you. There are days when it's hard to hold on, it's hard to keep putting one foot in front of the other, and it's certainly hard to believe that God really is looking out for you.

Yet when we look at our options, it's not hard to see that God truly is our only choice. He is the one who sticks closer than a brother when everyone else walks away.

We live in a corrupt and failing society, we are surrounded by those who have no interest in our needs, but rather, they put themselves before all else.

As much as we would like to believe the opposite, trusting in government, banks, and powerhouses is never going to help us through the hard times. Believing for the best in those things will never amount to our fears being relieved or our hopes being secured.

Unfortunately, the same goes for putting our trust in other people, it doesn't always work out the way we may like it to. It's not that those we trust in necessarily are bad people, or purposely hurt us, but things happen, feelings change, circumstances unfold.

Where does that leave us?

With God!

He is our ever-present help in time of need, He is our fortress, our strong tower, and our rock. He is the one we can lean on, depend on, and trust in. No matter what situation we find ourselves in, God is our hope.

As you walk through your difficult days, as you journey through hard things, I would encourage you to put your hope, your security, and your trust not in man, but only in God.

Prayer

Father God, I thank you that I can place my hope and my trust in you, knowing that you will never leave me or forsake me. My heart will always be secure in your perfect love.

Help me not to look to others for my self-worth, but to believe only in you and your truth. Give me wisdom to see the lies and deceptions that are so often brandished around as reality and fact, when we know they are just the works of the devil.

Help me to keep my eyes fixed on you, and not to be led astray by all that demands my attention, but rather let me be steadfast in holding onto your promises and being led by your Word.

Lord, I pray that you help me to trust you, to take my eyes off myself, to let go of my fear and my doubts, and to fully embrace you as my only source of hope.

When the days look dark, and anxiety threatens to steal my peace, dear Jesus, I pray that you would be my all in all, my more than enough, and the rock on which I stand.

Amen.

In Every Circumstance

Psalm 34:1 (NCV)
'I will praise the Lord at all times; His praise is always on my lips'.

The book of Psalms is full of honour, glory and blessing towards the Lord. It is an outcry of praise amid every circumstance.

There is no one better than David to have written about praising God at all times, and in every circumstance, for we know that David's life seemed to be an endless story of trouble and hardship, yet through it all He loved God with the most incredible steadfastness. No matter how much trouble he seemed to be in, and there was a lot, he never stopped giving glory to God for all He had done.

We are to praise God at all times, not just in the good times. We are to praise Him when all seems lost, when we don't know what to do, when our hearts are shattered, and when there seems to be no hope left.

It is during these times, the times when we struggle, the times when we feel like we are alone on our journey, that we find it hard to sing out His praises. It is when our soul feels crushed that we are hard pressed to find reason to glorify God and to honour Him with our lips, our hearts, and our lives.

Yet, it is then that we need to do it the most.

Hebrews 13:15 talks about bringing a 'sacrifice of praise'. This is giving honour and glory to God when it doesn't feel natural, when it's the last thing we want to do. But it's when we honour Him with our first fruits, when we give from our emptiness, and when we offer all that we are, that we are the closest to Him.

Jesus gave all that He was for us, how could we refuse to do the same? How can we hold back when we know that He held back nothing from us, but rather He sacrificed His all for our sake?

Today I would encourage you, no matter what you are going through, no matter what the shape of your heart, offer up your praise to God. Glorify Him for all that He has done, all He has given, and all that He is. Let His praise be always on your lips.

Prayer

Father God, I thank you for who you are, for what you do, and for what you mean to me.

You are my hope, my defender, the one I can run to, and the one who stands closer than a brother. You see into the depths of who I am, you know my every thought, and you continue to love me despite the state of my heart.

God, I am so grateful that you 'get me', I don't have to put on a show or pretend to be something I'm not, I can come to you just as I am and I know that will be enough, I know that you will draw me close and hold me tight.

Lord, may my lip always be ready to praise you, that regardless of my circumstances, may I always offer you my heart and honour you with all I do.

Father, in my every day, may you always be my everything.

Amen.

Watch Your Tongue

We have all had that moment when we have uttered words, and as soon as they have left our mouths, we've instantly wished we could take them back. We've said something in haste, something hurtful, or spiteful, or just downright rude, and we have known that it was wrong, yet it's too late to do anything about it.

Every day we can speak blessing or curses. We can speak life or death. We make the choice to be kind, or to be unkind.

We need to guard our tongues and be careful with what we choose to say, we need to hold back and refrain from just blurting out everything we think, instead, we need to weigh up whether the words we speak are going to cause damage to those we are speaking to.

It takes a bigger person to watch their words, rather than the person who gives their full opinion on every matter. The bigger person will count the cost, will value the relationship, and will seek to shield those they are talking to, rather than just giving in to the desire to make themselves feel heard.

There is a time for laying out the truth, for telling it how it is, and for sharing our version of events, but even in doing this, God requires that we do it in love. We need to prayerfully consider how we approach certain subjects, and we need to offer grace and mercy to others when we know we will be broaching difficult or sensitive topics.

Women are incredibly skilled in the art of conversation and discussion, but also in verbal warfare. We learn at an early age the ability to thrash out every problem by talking it through. It starts at the beginning of our journey as young girls and continues to grow into adulthood. However, we also learn how to use our words as weapons, and with them we wound each other, sometimes this is done accidently, and at other times it's intentional.

God wants us to use our words to build others up, to encourage, to strengthen and to love.

This week I would encourage you to ask God to keep a guard over your mouth and ask that He would give you the words that He has for you to speak.

Prayer

Lord Jesus, I pray that you would keep a guard over my mouth, that you would help me to hold my tongue when there is so much I want to say. Help me to remember that not every thought I have needs to be verbally shared, and that sometimes it's ok to just be silent.

Father, may my words bring hope and healing, may I always work towards unity, and may I speak with love to all those you bring across my path. Help me to choose my words wisely, and to find ways to uplift and encourage others.

Remind me that when I have nothing nice to say, then it's better to say nothing at all. If my words will wound, then let me hold them close and stay quiet rather than speak out and cause upset and distress.

Speak in me and through me, let those who spend time with me know that I am of you, let them see you, and hear you in all that I do and say. May my words speak life, not death.

Jesus, I pray your wisdom over every word I speak.

Amen.

The Walls Of Jericho

Hebrews 11:30 (NIV)
By faith the walls of Jericho fell, after the army
had marched around them for seven days.

Throughout the bible God has given instructions that seemingly don't make any sense, yet the outcome has been miraculous. All that He has asked for is that complete faith is placed in Him.

The battle of Jericho is no different.

God doesn't tell Joshua to go to war and fight against the Israelites, but rather He tells him to take his army, and walk around the walled city once a day for six days. Then on the seventh day they are to walk around the city seven times, blowing the trumpet as they march. On the seventh time they are to give one long blow of the trumpet and when the people hear this sound the army are to give a large shout, and the walls will come crashing down.

Can you imagine how the Israelites would have felt?

They had been terrified of Joshua and his army, yet when they see them just walking around the city, they would have been completely bewildered. Then the unthinkable happens, God steps in, the walls crumble and the victory is won.

Our God is the God of miracles, He is the God of victory, He is the God who moves in ways we could never imagine. He calls us to have faith and trust Him with every situation in our lives. He asks that we believe him for the answer, that we don't doubt Him, but rather we follow His leading, no matter how crazy it might seem.

If the walls you're praying for haven't come down yet, if your Jericho is still standing strong, don't give up. Keep praying, keep believing, and keep trusting God for the outcome. It's faith that will bring the walls down, keep placing your faith in the one 'who can do exceedingly, abundantly more than we can ask or think' (Ephesians 3:20).

Have faith that God will give you the victory for your Jericho, don't give up, as you journey in prayer, march to the beat of His drum, blow the trumpet of praise and keep going until the walls come down.

Prayer

Lord Jesus, give me a faith like that of Joshua, that I might hear your voice and follow in all that you have instructed. Help me to not fall into doubt when I don't understand what is happening, but rather let me continue to trust you more.

God, I give you my Jericho, I stand with open arms as I hand you the burdens of my heart. You see the tears I have cried, the anxiety I have felt, and the heartache I have endured, Lord, I give it all to you.

As I lay it all down, I ask that you bring victory. I ask that your power would be outworked, and that your will would be done. God give me faith over fear, strengthen my trust in you.

As I raise my hands to praise you, I pray for an infilling of your spirit, that you would give me a renewed vigour, and that I would stand strong in my commitment to follow you. May I not lean on my own understanding but believe in all that you speak out as truth. Let me wholly live for you.

Amen.

Be Slow To Anger

Proverbs 19:11 (AMP)
Good sense and discretion make a man slow to anger, and it is
his honour and glory to overlook a transgression or an offense
(without seeking revenge and harbouring resentment).

This scripture can certainly seem like a lot and maybe just a little hard to swallow!

When we are hurt, or treated badly, our first, second or third reaction is to become angry, and to want to retaliate against the one who has wronged us. We want to fight back, to have the last say and to repay our transgressor.

It's never easy to forgive and forget, to turn the other cheek, to let go and move on. It's just not in our nature to stand down, to overlook what was aimed at us, and not seek retribution.

Yet Proverbs tells us that 'good sense makes us slow to anger', which means that we just sit with the situation, we don't plough on making plans for revenge, but we use discretion, and, in our maturity, we hold our tongue, we show restraint, and we let it go.

None of this is ever easy, and in our own strength it's almost impossible, but the more we mature in our Christian journey, we know we have a God who will walk with us through the hurt, the disappointment, the anger, and the want for vengeance.

Holding a grudge is like walking around with an open wound, at any given moment it can fester and ooze, leaving a mess in its wake. When we carry around anger and offense, not dealing with it quickly and correctly, the aftereffects can permeate into every area of our lives leaving a trail of disaster behind it.

Today I want to encourage you, for the sake of your own peace and your relationship with God, let go of all the hurts and the anger, forgive those who have wronged you, and without seeking revenge, show good sense and discretion in all that you do.

Prayer

Father God, help me to be more like you, not looking for retribution, but turning the other cheek and letting it all go.

Help me to seek reconciliation before revenge, to find common ground, and to be the one looking for solutions rather than responding in a way that brings you no glory.

Jesus, I pray that your spirit would live within me, that I would be a peacemaker, and that I would choose love over being right in every situation. Help me to forgive, even when it costs me everything, when it breaks my heart, and when I know that I am not the one in the wrong, remind me that because of who you are, I can learn to let it go.

Holy Spirit, give me the wisdom to know when to speak, and when to be silent. Let me know the difference between saying what you would have me to say, and speaking out from a heart of hurt and anger. Teach me to hold my tongue and to bide my time.

God, give me good sense, let me not be led by my own selfish ambitions, my desire to be right, and my determination to stand my ground, but help me to know when to turn the other cheek, and walk away.

Lord, I pray for more of you, and less of me.

Amen.

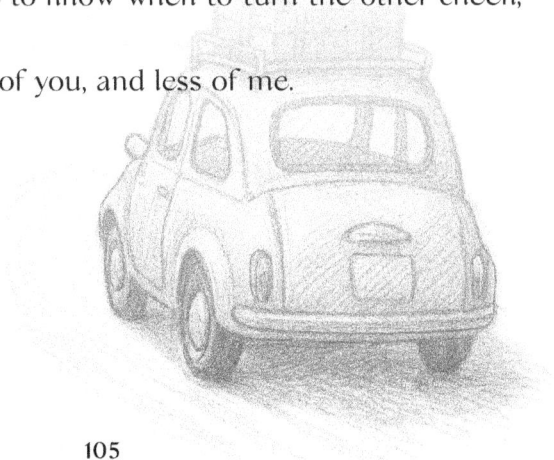

His Love Never Quits

Psalm 118:1-4 (MSG)
Thank God because He's good, because His love never quits.
Tell the world, Israel, "His love never quits."
And you, clan of Aaron, tell the world, "His love never quits."
And you who fear God, join in, "His love never quits."

Four times in this scripture we read the words 'His love never quits'. If ever we needed to believe that God is for us, that He cares about us, that He will be with us in all situations, we have our proof right here.

Regardless of all else, no matter what is happening in our world, irrespective of what we have done, God will never give up on us, He will never stop loving us. He will be with us through thick and thin, wherever we may journey in life. In the good and the bad times, even when we mess up, even when we walk away, even when we are knee deep in sin, God's love for us will never quit.

We often find that worldly love is conditional, it is temporary, it is based on feelings, and it can be taken away when we don't measure up.

It is the type of love that still leaves us longing, it can leave us lonely and without hope that we are protected, cared for or held. Love is a word that is used flippantly to get results, and to make us believe that if we look or behave a certain way then we are acceptable, and therefore loveable.

God's love is for us regardless of how we look, how we behave or how hard we try. His love is passionate and unrelenting. It will chase after us, it will restore us, and it will deeply satisfy us.

I would encourage you today to let God remind you of what you mean to Him, let Him show you how deeply He cares about you, how He would go to the ends of the earth for you, and how He will never quit loving you.

Prayer

Lord, I thank you for your great, all-consuming love. I thank you that your love for me will never quit, it will never give in, give up, or give it all away. I thank you that when all else fades, your love never will.

Father God you are the creator of love, it is because of your great love towards us that you gave your son Jesus, that you allowed Him to become a sacrifice for our sake. Lord, there is no greater love than laying down one's life for another, and this is what you did for us.

Lord, I thank you that your love for me is passionate, it's all consuming, it's not temperamental or dependant on conditions, but rather it is relentless in its pursuit. Lord, never let me forget just how strong your love is toward me.

On my weakest days, my darkest days, and in those moments when I feel lost, Lord, remind me once again of your love, remind me that I am not alone, but that you are with me, standing beside me and holding me close.

Lord, thank you for who you are and how you love.

Amen.

Keep Going

1 Chronicles 28:20 (GNT)
King David said to his son Solomon, "Be confident and determined.
Start the work and don't let anything stop you. The Lord God, whom
I serve, will be with you. He will not abandon you, but he will stay
with you until you finish the work to be done on his Temple."

When God leads us into the work that He has for us, into the plan and purpose that He has, then He will be with us each step of the way. He won't abandon us halfway through our journey, He won't change His mind about what He has promised, and He won't leave us on our own to work it out. God has proven Himself to us time and again, He is with us for the long-haul, from here to eternity, so we need not worry whether He will keep showing up, of course He will, that's who God is.

When I first started to write my books, I was slightly terrified that God wouldn't walk with me through each step that I was taking. I worried that somehow, I would be left faltering and not sure of what to do next. But in His goodness, God was right beside me each step of the way.

He just needed me to keep going, to do the work that was required, and then He would take care of the rest.

I think each of us struggle with what the next step will be, we're scared of putting in the hard yards in case it amounts to nothing. We live in fear that God will leave us to sort out all the details on our own when we so desperately need Him to walk with us.

In this verse King David is talking to his son, he is reminding him that the God that he serves will be with him each step of the way, he is encouraging Solomon to keep going, not to give up, but to be confident and determined in all that he is doing to complete what God has called him to.

If God has called you to something, keep going, push on, and do all that is required. Don't give up out of fear or worry or lack of confidence, but know that the God who called, is the same God who equips.

Stay strong and do the work.

Prayer

Lord, I thank you for that which you have called me to, for the work you have planned for me, and the purpose that I am to fulfill. Lord, I thank you that I do not need to fear because I know that you are with me. I am not walking this path alone, but together we walk hand in hand.

Father, for the times I have doubted you, for the moments I have been overwhelmed and struggled to hear your voice or understand your plan, forgive me for my weakness. For the many times I have put aside what I know you have asked me to do, when I have ignored your whisper, and I have ploughed headfirst into my own agenda, God, I pray you forgive me for my determination to do things my own way.

Lord Jesus, just as you have been with each of the disciples in their times of doubt, or distress, or unfaithfulness, I pray that you would be with me. You would continue to offer me your patience and your grace, you would hold onto me as I step out of the boat and walk towards you, filled with both fear and faith.

God, give me the strength to do what you have called me to do, help me not to waver but to focus only on your plan and purpose, leaning not on my own understanding, but Lord, only on you.

Amen.

Even In Suffering

Have you ever wondered how Job survived the most devastating and soul-destroying years of his life? Have you ever thought why didn't he blame God, or at the very least, doubt Him for all that had happened?

We read in Job that God allows the devil to annihilate Job's life, taking his possessions, his family, his health and everything else he holds dear, the only thing that the devil can't take is Job's life. In and through this, the devil waits for Job to curse God and blame Him for all that has taken place. However, this never happens. Job is heartbroken, he is desolate, a man destroyed, but not once does he blame God.

I think of how I would feel if everything I had worked for was gone, if everyone I loved was put to death, and if my health was stripped away, I would go through all the emotions from anger to devastation, and I would certainly want answers from God as to why.

Yet, Job was a man who had journeyed a long time with God, he knew the character of God, and he knew that He could be trusted. Job knew that he came naked from his mother's womb, and naked he would return, he knew that the Lord gave, and the Lord could take away. There was nothing to blame God for.

What an incredible testament of faith! The devil could do nothing to sway Job for he was grounded in his relationship with God. Even when his friends bemoaned his very existence, Job refused to bow down and blame God for anything, rather he clung to Him in his moment of need and cried out to Him in deep despair.

As each of us walk out our own faith journey, we are faced with many things that try to destroy us. There are hurts, betrayals, losses, and deceptions, each one of these things could have us crying out to God asking why He let this happen. But, considering Job's story, I would encourage you to go to God in worship before anything else, take on the mantle of Job and give God glory rather than blame.

Prayer

Lord, there is so much I can learn, even when it appears too hard, when it is totally foreign to me and completely out of my comfort zone. I thank you so much for the stories of the saints, for those who went before me, those who suffered and yet continued to hold onto you.

Father, I pray that my attitude would be found to be like that of Job, that in the face of every type of heartbreak, I would not run to you with blame, but with praise. That I would recognise that all that I have is from you, and at any stage this can be taken away.

Help me to never hear the voice of others over your voice, may your words be the ones that are written on my heart, so that I can call on them on the days I need to hear and speak your truth. Help me to discern what is right from what appears right, knowing that that your way is always the way I should go.

Lord, when I feel overwhelmed, when the days are dark, when I can't see any reason for what's happening around me, draw me close, comfort me, and help me to find my way. Let me lean not on my own understanding, but fully place my trust in you, the one who knows best.

Lord, show me the way
Amen

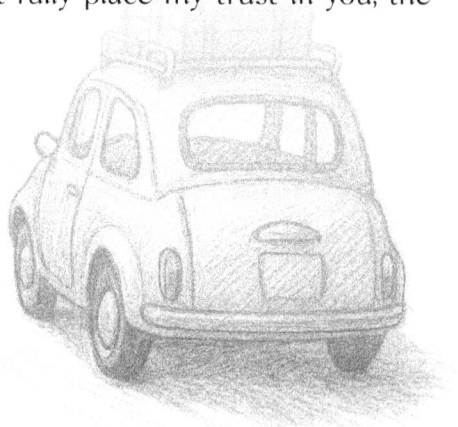

God Is Our Waymaker

Isaiah 43:19 (NIV)
See, I am doing a new thing! Now it springs up; do you not perceive it?
I am making a way in the wilderness and streams in the wasteland.

How often do we feel stuck? We feel like we are forever trapped in 'Groundhog Day', and that we are living our lives in a series of repeats.

We can sometimes feel like nothing good could possibly come from the ground we are standing on, the path we are walking, or the journey we are taking.

Yet God tells us that He is doing a new thing, that He is making a way when it looks like there is no way. He is moving through the wilderness, and He is creating beautiful and refreshing streams in what was once wasteland.

Sometimes our lives feel just like a barren wilderness, we feel dry and empty. Our bodies are parched, and our souls are thirsty, wishing, hoping, and praying for more.

Each of us has known days when we have craved for something different, when we have longed for new beginnings and open-ended possibilities.

Today, is your new beginning, this is your opportunity to walk with God into His plan and purpose for your life. He says He is doing a 'new thing', that means He has something in store for you that you haven't experienced before, something that is out of the ordinary, not the same, and altogether better than what you've already experienced.

God is the creator of all things, He is the beginning and the end, He is the way maker and the hope of tomorrow. Just because your life has seemed empty or stuck until now, that doesn't mean it will continue that way. When God opens doors, they are for your good, they will provide opportunities of blessing and will be streams in what was once wasteland.

Partner with Him today in the new thing that He has planned for you and walk with Him out of the wilderness and into your promised land.

Prayer

Lord Jesus, I thank you that today is a new day, that I can start again, and that my story is not over. I thank you that together we are walking into my next chapter.

Lord, I am so grateful that although I may feel stuck, I may feel lost, and there are many days that I feel trapped, in you there is always a way out of the desert, and into the promised land.

Jesus, you are my restorer, the lifter of my head, and the hope of my tomorrow. I live in a place of thankfulness that you lead me, not allowing me to fend for myself, but you journey with me towards all that you have planned.

God, I thank you that you are the creator of heaven and earth, you know the beginning from the end, and you are the author of my story. There is nothing that takes place that you don't allow, and you give me grace to walk through the hardest of days into the most beautiful place of peace.

Jesus, help me to trust you, to remember your promises and to rely on your truth, remind me of who you, and who I am in you, a child held safely in your arms of love.

Amen.

Free Indeed

John 8:36 (NIV)
If the Son sets you free, you are will be free indeed.

---

love this scripture because it is explicitly clear. If we are set free by Jesus, then that is exactly what we are, we are free.

It doesn't say that in certain circumstances we can be free, we aren't just free when we feel good, when the stars align, when life is going well. We are free indeed. The word indeed is used here to emphasize and confirm the previous words, it's like the exclamation mark at the end of the sentence. See it in big bold letters – FREE.

Jesus wants us to live our lives free from everything that holds us backs or ties us in knots. What He doesn't want is for us to be crippled by fear, or doubt, or insecurities. He doesn't want us to shy away from being bold, from exercising our faith, or from spreading His Word.

He wants us to take a journey with Him where we are our true selves, where we can let go of all that has held us in chains or keeps us from moving forward. He wants us to step out, be all that He created us to be, and live our best lives.

Freedom in and through Christ is our greatest hope, it's our weapon and it's our gift. It was paid for in blood, sweat and tears. It was bestowed upon us in love, and it unshackles us from a life of imprisonment.

When a prisoner's prison sentence is voided and the prisoner is set free, it is called a pardon. That is what Jesus has done for us. He didn't just give us a 'stay' which has a limitation of time, and is a temporary reprieve, but we have received a full 'pardon', His full forgiveness. He has untied our handcuffs, He has unlocked our cells, and He has given us a second chance.

A chance to love, to live, and to glorify Him, we get to start again, to be renewed, and to be set free. We get to move forward in our freedom.

Because of this, we can live out our God given destiny, to shine as we were created, and to use who we are to make a difference in the life of others.

Use your freedom well.

Prayer

Lord Jesus, I thank you that because of you I can live in freedom. I can know that my life has meaning and purpose, and that I can boldly step into all you have planned for me.

I am so grateful for the gift of life, a life that is not bogged down by fear, or doubt, or anxiety, but rather, a life that is filled with hope for tomorrow.

Jesus, thank you for setting me free from everything that tries to steal my joy, and destroy my peace. Because of all you have done, I can rise above whatever the world tries to throw at me, and can claim your victory, through the power of your name.

Father God, help me to share this story of freedom, to speak into the lives of others, and offer them the gift that has been offered to me. Let me shine your light so that others will see you through me and seek you out with diligence and determination.

Lord, may I never bow down to the darkness that tries to overwhelm me, but let me remain strong in you, let me hold tight to your truth, and walk uprightly in your ways.

Today, Lord Jesus, may I live my life wholly sold out for you. Amen.

Don't Look Back

Genesis 19:26 (GNT)
But Lot's wife looked back and was turned into a pillar of salt.

The story of Lot, his wife, and their children, fleeing from their home in Sodom, under the protection of God, is one of grace and mercy.

God had sent His angels to destroy the evil and filth that had overtaken the cities of Sodom and Gomorrah, but out of His love for Abraham, He offered an escape route to Lot and his family. He gave them an opportunity to take a journey that would lead them to a place of safety.

The angels of the Lord said to them in V17 'Flee for your lives! Don't look back.'

During this situation, the chaos and the terror, one would think that the family, hearing the words of the angels would make a run for it, not stopping to look around or look back. But not Lot's wife, she had one final glance behind her, and in doing so she was turned into a pillar of salt.

Why did she look back? What did she see? Was she concerned for those left behind, her friends and extended family?

When Lot's wife looked back, she changed the course of history for her own small family. Her choice left her husband alone to care for their children and left her two daughters without a mother, these girls then went on make decisions they might never have made if she had done as God instructed.

For each of us as women, there are many times we look back. We look at what could have been, we look at what we should have said or done, we look at missed opportunities and we look at the choices we made, good or bad.

When we look back, we focus on what is gone, rather than on what is still to come. We look at the past, instead of the opportunities that God will bring into our future. By looking back, we deny God the chance to bring something beautiful out of something hard.

Today I would encourage you not to look back, but to keep your eyes on the path ahead of you, and trust that God is leading you where He wants you to go.

Prayer

Father God, help me to keep my eyes on you, to focus on all you're calling me to, rather than all that is behind me. Help me not to look back on all that has past, but to watch and look forward to all that is still ahead.

Lord, I thank you for the journey you have taken me on, for the ups and downs of life, the highs and the lows. I am grateful for every moment where I have been able to rely on you, grow my faith, and learn to trust you more than ever before.

Jesus, help me to hear your voice, and to follow your direction. Give me the wisdom to know when to move, and when to stay. Help me lean not on my own understanding, but to follow you always. Remind me that I can trust you in all things, and that my hope in you will never be shaken.

God, when you call me out of situations, help me to move swiftly, even when I don't understand what's going on, or where I'm heading to. Let me know that you always have my best at heart, and you will journey with me wherever I go.

Amen.

Surrender Your Anxiety

Psalm 46:10 (TPT)
Surrender your anxiety. Be silent and stop your
striving and you will see that I am God.

nxiety can be an overwhelming, life-threatening, and fear inducing emotion that robs us of all peace.

It can sneak up on us when we least expect it, day or night, and in the most unusual of circumstances. We can be going about our day to day, taking one step at a time on our journey through life, and suddenly we may find ourselves in a sweat, worrying without good cause, and allowing all sense to go out the window.

God wants us to surrender our anxiety to Him. He wants us to let go of what is holding us prisoner, and to allow Him to be our peace in the storm.

He tells us to stop our striving, our working in vain, and our endless pushing on during trying circumstances. He wants us to be silent and to be still. He wants us to rest in Him, to take time out, to realign our thoughts and to focus on who He is, rather than on what is going on around us.

For us to see God, we need to train the eyes of our heart to seek Him out, to put aside all else, to shut down negativity and fear and doubt, and to only gaze upon Him.

In our moments of anxiety, and during times of striving, when we are continually driven to be active, we need to learn the art of stopping. We need to consciously slow down our thinking, be prepared to say no, and to allow our lives to become uncluttered and free.

It's in the quiet that we can hear God speak, it's in the waiting that He can renew us, and it's when we hand everything over to Him, that we are finally able to see that He is Lord over all.

In the busyness of your day, surrender all that you are and all that you have to Him, be silent in His presence and see that He is God.

Prayer

Father God, I thank you that you are the source of hope that you are the giver of life, and that you hold all my days in your hands.

Lord, you can see the beginning to the end, you see my today and you know my tomorrow. Help me to find peace in knowing that you are with me on the good days and the bad, that no matter what is happening in my world, you are my defender.

God, I hand over all my anxiety to you, all the things that keep me up at night, the worries I have, the fears for tomorrow and every small detail that fills me with stress. Dear God, I now lay these at your feet in surrender.

Help me to let go, to trust without reservation, and to hold onto the truth of who you are. Remind me Lord that you are sovereign, that you are faithful, and that in you I can stand strong and courageous.

Thank you, Jesus, for being my lifeline, for being my anchor in the storm, and the one I can rely on. Thank you that your perfect love casts out all fear, and that because of you I can walk into tomorrow with my head held high, and my eyes set on you.

Amen.

Be Prepared

The Bible makes it very clear that we don't know when Jesus will return, we don't know the moment He will choose to sound the trumpet and make His triumphant re-entry amongst us.

There are many who claim to know the date and time, who would have us believe that everything that is currently happening in the world is a sign that we are in the final chapter of life.

Yet we really don't know.

What we do know, is that we need to be prepared, we need to ensure that we have our hearts set on Him, that we are walking with Him and have a good relationship with Him. We need to know that we have done our best, that we have shared our faith, the good news of Christ, with all those around us. None of us want to have any regrets, and on the day that we see Him face to face, we want to hear Him say "Well done good and faithful servant" (Matthew 25:19).

So often on our journey through life, we get caught up in the things of the world, we become distracted by the little things, and we lose sight of the bigger picture. We often don't remember our true calling, our deepest love, and the purpose of all that we do.

Jesus should be our beginning and end. He should be our first thought in the morning, and our last thought at night. It should be His Word that we run to each day, fully soaking ourselves in learning more about Him, and spending time listening to and hearing from Him.

When we see Him appearing on the clouds there should be no moment of hesitation within us, no sudden dread, no fear, and no regrets. Our eyes should look up in expectation and excitement, and our hearts should leap for joy within us. The day of our Saviour's return should fill us with immense happiness, and we should be exuberant about His appearance.

I would encourage you today you to give yourself the best opportunity to meet with Jesus, hand your life 100% over to Him, knowing that at any time, He could come to take you home.

Prayer

Jesus, I thank you that this world is not my forever home, this is not my final dwelling place. One day I will go to be with you, and life will become what you always planned for it to be, perfect.

Lord, I pray that you help me to be prepared, help me to hold loosely to all that I have here on earth, but rather always storing up for myself treasures in heaven.

Father, I thank you that when the day comes, when I am called home, that you will find me to have been both 'good and faithful'. Lord, I want to be able to look at you, face to face, knowing that I have done all that I could do, and I am now ready to meet my maker.

Lord, while I still have breath in my lungs, give me opportunities to share you with others. To show courage in the face of adversity, and be willing to take a stand for truth, pointing others towards you.

Jesus, help me not to be distracted, not to get caught up in the day to day of life, but to focus on the one thing that really matters, and that is being in the right place with you. Lord, I ask now that you help me to fix my gaze on things above, and to walk wholly in your ways.

Amen.

In The Waiting

Micah 7:7 (NLT)
As for me, I look to the Lord for help. I wait confidently for
God to save me, and my God will certainly hear me.

We all know that waiting can be hard. It's not easy to hold out for something when we live in a world where everything is instant. Where no matter what we want, it's easily accessible, and can often be had by the click of a finger.

It's not easy to come to terms with the fact that what we want is not going to happen quickly, when the thing we have longed for will require more from us than just instant gratification. It can be very difficult to hold onto hope and believe for something when time seems to be dragging on, and the thing we want most in the world doesn't seem to be happening.

The word 'wait' is mentioned 139 times in the bible, which tells me that God knew what we would be going through. He understood that there would be many times when we would need to hold back, to be patient, to sit in the stillness and to put our hope and trust in Him. It is

His greatest desire that we don't just give in to all our wants, but we wait for His best, that we don't choose the first option because it looks easy, but we prayerfully seek His plan and purpose for our lives.

God wants us to wait confidently in Him, to not waver in knowing that He is our safe place, our rock, and our fortress. He is the one we can run to and find shelter. God wants us to hope in Him for our future, and to trust that He knows what is best.

He wants us to enjoy the journey, but that can sometimes mean we need to accept that not everything will go as smoothly as we hope, the progress may be slow, and the destination may look different to what we were expecting. Because of this, it is so important for us to remember that God's ways and His timing can be so different to ours.

I would encourage you today to seek and put Him first, knowing that He is with you in the waiting, and that even when it's hard, God is the one who will hear you, help you, and save you.

Prayer

Lord Jesus, give me the strength to hold tight as I wait on you, help me to stay strong and remain focused on the prize. Give me an extra portion of faith as I trust and believe in you for my promised land.

Lord, walk with me I pray, let me lean not on my own understanding, but continue to trust in you, even when I can't see what's happening, when the road ahead looks long and I'm weary from the journey.

Jesus, I know that you are in control, I know that you have my best interest at heart, and that you only want what is right for me. On the days when I struggle to see this, when I give in to doubt and depression, continue to carry me and show me how much you love me.

Father, as I stand in the hallway and wait for the door to open, may I remain positive, trusting and faithful towards you. May I always believe in who you are and what you say, not being easily swayed by my circumstances.

Lord, I place all my hope in you, I know that tomorrow is promised to no one, but each day is a gift, remind me of this on those days when I don't appreciate all that I have.

Today, Jesus, may I walk in sync with you, knowing that no matter how long I wait, no matter how hard the trial, and no matter what the outcome, you Lord are my portion and my peace.

Amen.

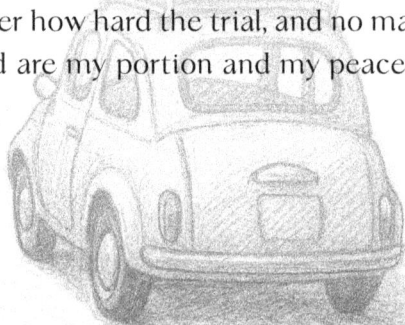

It's Ok To Rest

Genesis 2:2 (NIV)
By the seventh day God had finished the work He had been
doing; so on the seventh day He rested from all His work.

A few years ago, I had the joy of taking small groups of ladies away to the beach for Christian women's retreats.

It was a beautiful time of refreshment, of giving the women space to just stop, be still, and rest with God. A time where they didn't need to rush from one activity to another, but they could just relax and be renewed.

As women we are constantly on the go, we wear our busyness like a badge of honour, however, this was never God's blueprint for how our lives should look. When He created the earth and all that was in it, He rested. He didn't find more and more things to do, He didn't continually work His fingers to the bone, but He stopped, He looked at all He had done, and He was pleased.

We too need to stop, we need to take time out on our journey to enjoy the fruits of our labour, we need to put aside all that has kept us busy, and just rest.

All of us need to find time in our schedules to be quiet, to put our feet up, to soak in God's presence and to give Him the opportunity to whisper into our hearts. This is the reality of Sabbath, yet most of us don't make it a priority. We don't pull back, or say no, we rarely set boundaries, yet for the sake of our health, physical and spiritual, we need to learn that self-love includes drawing away, finding peace and resting.

Jesus called His disciples away to a quiet place, He knew they needed time out, they had been bombarded by people and they just needed some space.

Today He is calling you away also, He is whispering into your heart that it's time to slow down, it's time to refocus, and it's time to learn the art of being still.

I would encourage you to hear His voice, to make space in your life for rest, and to let Him lead you into the quiet place that He is calling you.

Prayer

Lord Jesus, open my ears to hear your still small voice, open my heart to be ready to receive all that you have to say, even when I find it difficult to listen to.

As you draw me closer to you, help me to be obedient to all that you are calling me away from, all the distractions that steal my peace and rob me of precious time with you. Help me to set my priorities and put boundaries in place for the things that try to take over and set themselves up as idols in my life.

Jesus, may you always be my focus, the one I live for, and the sole purpose of all that I am. May I choose you above all else each day, and set my heart to follow you in all that I do.

Holy Spirit, as you call me into a time of rest, help me to not fight against it, but rather to embrace all that it means, to be willing to slow down and to let go of all things that are not of you.

Today as I sit in silence, as I contemplate your presence in my life, Lord Jesus, I thank you for your grace, your peace, and your rest. May I never take for granted the blessing of all that you give.

Amen

Faithfulness

Lamentations 3:22-23 (NLT)
The faithful love of the Lord never ends! His mercies never cease.
Great is His faithfulness; His mercies begin afresh each morning.

We live in a world that brandishes the word 'love' around and strips it of all meaning.

We have become a people who have no concept of faithfulness, and we struggle to remain true to those closest to us.

We can see in the world that marriage is no longer held to the standard by which God designed it, with couples falling in and out of love at regular intervals, and lives ruined by the unfaithfulness of one partner to the other.

The only true love that we can hold onto is the love that God has for us. His love is faithful and never ending. It isn't based on our behaviour, our looks, our defining moments, or our ability to love Him back, but it is purely based on His immeasurable and devoted heart towards us.

God begins each day by pouring out His mercy on us, He holds nothing back. He doesn't remember our iniquities from yesterday, He doesn't hold a grudge over something we may or may not have done, and He never reminds us of the many areas where we may have failed. However, what He does do, is forgive us. He lets go of all that we have done, simply putting it out of His mind, and He chooses to move forward, loving us each step of the way.

Right from the beginning of our journey in life, when God looks at us, He does so through eyes of grace, He is not looking at us in judgement or holding against us all our many sins, but He is looking at us the way that a groom looks at his bride, with eyes of adoration and love. He is looking at us the way a mother looks at her newborn baby, with immense devotion and wonder. He sees who we are, and He is overwhelmed with affection and pride.

Remember this, God is faithful, and He loves you, today, tomorrow, and forever.

Prayer

Lord Jesus, I thank you for your faithful love, for your never-ending grace and for your mercy which surrounds me each day.

I am so grateful for your kindness, for the way you choose to see me, even when I can't see myself the same way. I am grateful for your forgiveness, that washes me clean, that removes my sin as far as the east is from the west.

Father God, you are my dwelling place, the home where my heart is safe, and my soul is at peace. I thank you that I can be refreshed and renewed in you, and that I am covered and hedged in on all sides.

Jesus, I thank you for your example of true love, I thank you for the cross, that you chose to lay down your life for me, and although I didn't deserve it, you did it anyway.

I thank you Lord that your love for me isn't defined by my behaviour, my looks, my attitude or position, but that before the beginning of time you set me apart and chose to love me, regardless of the cost. This is a love I can never repay and will always remain grateful for.

Thank you Jesus.

Amen.

From The Rising Of The Sun

Psalm 113:3 (NIV)
From the rising of the sun to the place where it sets,
the name of the Lord is to be praised.

For me, the morning begins with God. It's a time when the house is quiet, when there are no distractions, when in solitude I can meet with Him. Whether it's still dark or the sun is just rising, it's our time to start the day.

This is a time, when over coffee, I can read the Word, I can pray, I can pour my heart out, and I can listen for His still small voice, and prepare for the day ahead.

God wants us to start and end our days with Him. He wants us to give Him our time, to be fully engaged in relationship with Him, that we would come before Him with praise and thanksgiving.

So often our attitude determines how our day will look. We are led one way or the other by all that comes at us from morning till night. We are constantly bombarded by the needs and wants of others, the commitments of family or work, and the ongoing pressures of life. There is always something or someone who needs us in some way, who takes up our time, either physically, mentally or spiritually.

All of this can steal our peace, our joy, our hope, and our time with God. It can lead us into negativity, depression, hopelessness, and fatigue. It can rob us of all the blessings that God wants to pour out on us, as it saps the very life from us and drains us of all energy.

However, by giving God our first moments, by committing our day to Him, praising Him for all that He is doing and will continue to do, we are setting ourselves up for success. We are placing ourselves in the prime position to journey through our day prepared for all that may come our way.

I would encourage you today to make space for God, spend time with Him, offering Him your best. Praise Him from morning till night and allow Him to guide and lead you in all that you do.

Prayer

Lord Jesus, I give you my day, I offer up to you all that I am and ask that you walk with me through all that comes my way.

Give me a gentle and teachable spirit, that I might walk in peace with those around me, that my attitude would remain pure and that my tongue would be held when there is so much I may want to say.

Help me Lord to fix my eyes on you, to stay rooted in your truth, and to walk uprightly in every situation. Remind me of my position and keep my heart in check that I would bring honour to you in all I say and do.

Lord, as I spend time each morning reading your Word, listening for your still small voice, and giving space to the Holy Spirit, prepare me for all that comes my way. Fill me with your wisdom so that I would speak carefully and live wisely.

Jesus, I pray that I would decrease so that you may increase, fill me to overflowing with all that you are, be my ever-present help, and walk with me through this day

Amen.

First And Last

Revelation 22:13 (NLT)
I am the Alpha and the Omega, the Beginning
and the End, the First and the Last.

Before the beginning of time, God existed, there was never a moment where He was not omnipotent and all powerful.

Creation came into being because of Him, He breathed life into everything that now has breath. There was no meteorite that hit the earth and suddenly we all came to be, there was no big bang, we are not descendants of apes who underwent the process of natural selection. No, we are the handiwork of God, His magnificent creation.

Before the mountains and the valleys, the oceans and the rivers, the vastness of the desert, there was God. It was Him who created all.

He has been with every generation from the beginning and will be until the very end. He has watched over our forefathers, our ancestors and all those who came before us, just as He is now watching over us, and will then continue to watch over those who come after us, our children, and our children's children.

He has the final say on all things, for all things are held in His hands. He will be the judge and the jury; He will determine the outcome for those who have loved Him and those who haven't. He will be the one to either welcome us home, or say He never knew us. For He will be the Omega, the End and the Last. For when each of us breathe our final breath, the breath that He gave us, then we will stand before Him. It is then that our maker will determine our outcome, based on what we chose to do with the life He gave us.

The decisions we make today are not just frivolous and of no value, but rather they are all stepping stones to our final day, the day when we meet our maker face to face and our destiny is sealed.

For each of us to have our names in the book of life, we need to prepare our hearts, our souls, and our minds to meet the one who is the Alpha and Omega. No matter where your journey started, only you can determine where it finishes.

Have you made that decision today?

Prayer

Father, I thank you that before the beginning of time, you were God, you were the Alpha and the Omega.

Lord, you are the creator of all, you breathed life into the universe, you made something beautiful out of nothing at all, and you shaped us in your image. I am so thankful that we are not a mistake, but we are your creation, your perfect handiwork.

Lord, when the voices of the world talk of evolution, when they shout out that there is no God, but that we all just came to be, give me the words to shut them down, help me to be courageous in standing up for truth.

Remind me Lord that this is not my forever home, that life as I know it here will one day pass away, and then I will stand before you. Let all I do between now and then bring glory to you and bring me into a place of closeness with you.

Help me to always see the bigger picture, to not be weighed down by the day-to-day issues that continually come about, but help me to keep my focus on what truly matters, give me a heavenly perspective in all things.

Jesus, I am so grateful that you are the hope of the world, that because of you we can face tomorrow, and for all you are, I give thanks.

Amen.

Fertile Ground

Psalm 1:3 (NLT)
They are like trees planted along the riverbank, bearing fruit each
season. Their leaves never wither, and they prosper in all they do.

T
he environment that you place yourself in can either stifle your
growth, or it can take you from strength to strength. It can limit
you or it can take you to great heights, allowing you to spread
and grow more than you ever imagined.

When a tree is placed into the right soil, and given the right nutrients,
and the right amount of water, it has all that it needs to grow up strong
and healthy. If it is placed into a pot rather than into the ground, it will
never reach its full potential, for it is limited by the size of where it has
been planted.

The same can be said for us, the environment that we are in can
either help us to grow as Christians, or it can be detrimental for us. Our
nutrients can be found in the people we surround ourselves with, what
we allow to fill our minds, how we spend our days, and whether we pri-
oritise our time with God.

To yield fruit, trees need to be well fed and watered, they need to have deep roots, and plenty of sunshine to enable their growth. The journey from a young sapling to a full-bodied tree is determined by the care it receives. This too is so true for us, we need to be fed by the Word of God, we need the Holy Spirit, we need to be entrenched in biblical teaching, and we need valuable time with the Son.

When we place ourselves in pots, rather than in fertile ground, when we are in situations that are not right for us, we are limiting what God can do in our lives, and the growth that we can have. We are not giving ourselves the best environment to thrive, or to be strong and healthy.

I would encourage you today to look around you at where you are planted, make sure that you have all that you need for your fruit to grow, to ensure that your leaves do not wither, and that all that you do prospers.

Prayer

Lord, I pray for your perfect conditions, for fertile soil, for the right amount of watering, and for the best environment, that I might grow strong and healthy for you.

Father God, I want to be in the right place that you can grow me into the person you want me to be. I want to have the best opportunity to be vibrant and strong, to stand tall and to be fruitful.

I know that not every tree is healthy, and those who aren't are often pruned or cut down. God, I pray that you keep me healthy, that I would flourish under your hand, that I would move in whichever way you direct the wind, that I would be bendable and that my limbs would be able to endure whatever comes their way.

Lord, I ask that you take me from strength to strength, that I would not be stifled but would continue to grow, that my buds would blossom, and my fruit would be ripe. I pray that I would be an example of your workmanship to those around me.

Thank you, God, that I need not be stifled, but in you I can grow, not limiting myself, but flourishing under your hand.

Amen.

See The Best In Others

1 Thessalonians 5:15 (MSG)
*And be careful that when you get on each other's nerves
you don't snap at each other. Look for the best in each
other, and always do your best to bring it out.*

I t can be so easy to find fault in others, to see the flaws in someone else
and to be irritated by their behaviour.

It's easy to snap at those around us when we are tired or frustrated
or angry, and we can often be filled with annoyance towards those in our
closest circle.

Yet we are encouraged not to take the easy way out, not to just give
in to our feelings, not to act on them when we want to bite back, to have
the last word, or to withhold kindness from others.

We are told to look for the best in others. To see what God sees, to
look at our family and friends, or our colleagues and neighbours, through
rose-coloured glasses. To not focus on their faults, but rather to see them
the same way God sees them, as precious and priceless.

There are days when it can be hard to follow this advice, when loving others seems futile, when their actions leave us disappointed and hurt. It doesn't seem worth going the extra mile for them when they don't appreciate our efforts. Yet this is the very thing we are told to do. We are told to take the high road, to journey with them, and to love them unconditionally, just as Jesus would.

We are instructed to not only look for the best in others, but to bring that out of them. To work toward letting them shine in all that they do, to walk with them and encourage them to excel and to be the best that they can be.

We are not given permission to put down, to ridicule, to hold back or to stifle the growth in someone else, but rather, to do all that we can to bring them to the place where they are living their best life.

Today I would encourage you to love others the way God loves them, to not find fault, but to practise kindness and to do all you can to bring out the best in those around you.

Prayer

Lord Jesus, help me to love the way that you do, to put others first, to allow my needs to come second to those around me.

Give me a heart that is moved and broken for the lost, the lonely, the hurting and the wayward.

Help me to see others through your eyes, not to measure them by my standards, but by yours. Help me not criticize, put down, condemn or judge, but rather let me see them as an incredible creation of yours.

Father, when I place myself above others, remind me that each of us is beautiful and worthy in your eyes, that I am no better than anyone else, but you have made us all equal.

Help me to remember that it is only by your grace that I am where I am today, that if it hadn't been for you, I could very well be walking in the shoes of the very people I choose to look down upon.

God, I pray that my eyes would convey love and mercy rather than disdain and disgust. Let me only see the best in others, not the worst, and finally Lord, let me always remember, that I too am a sinner, saved by grace, your grace.

Amen.

Love In Action

This is such a challenging scripture, yet the basis of what all Christianity is built on, we are to love others not just with our words, but with our actions and deeds.

It's not enough to tell the broken that we are praying for them, but rather, we must be willing to go the extra mile for them, asking what they need and then being willing to help provide.

What have we got to offer those who desperately have needs, those without food or family or homes?

Jesus, in His time on earth, loved the unlovable, He spent time with those despised by others,

He held the hands of the sick and the dying. He didn't tell them to come back later, He didn't palm them off on someone else, but He got into the trenches with them, and He gave them what they needed.

We live in a world that is fixated on what others can do for us, rather than on what we can do for others, unfortunately we take more than we give. We choose not to journey with the needy, because it takes our time, our money, and our resources. It takes all the things we don't want to part with.

As Christians we need to take on the mind of Christ, we need to fill our hearts with His compassion and His great love for others. We need to remember His very words when He said to 'love others as ourselves'.

Our capacity to serve is only as great as we allow it to be. We all have opportunities to spend time with those less fortunate than ourselves, to open our homes to those in need, to seek out those who are hurting, those who are desperate for friendship and love. Our churches and communities are crying out for volunteers to help in one way or another.

Today I would encourage you to truly find out what it means to love, not just in words, but in action and in truth.

Prayer

Lord Jesus, forgive me for my selfish ways, for not being willing to put myself out, for not going the extra mile, and for not being your hands and feet to the world around me.

Lord, change my attitude so that I can be more in tune with you, help me to be willing to give of all I have, holding nothing in reserve. Give me a heart that breaks for the hurt, the lonely, the fallen and the lost.

Jesus, lead me to those who need you, open my eyes so that I see others the way you do. Help me not to judge, but to offer grace and mercy, to show kindness and compassion, and to be willing to walk the hard road with them.

God, break down the barriers I have put up regarding those who are different to me, those who have made choices that I find hard to understand, those who have walked a journey so unlike my own. Let me see them through your eyes and be open to loving them the way you do.

Holy Spirit, without you I can never make a difference, for it is you who softens my heart, gives me words of wisdom, and speaks truth. I pray that you would work in me, so that I might work with others.

Amen.

In Mourning And Dancing

Ecclesiastes 3:4 (NIV)
A time to weep and a time to laugh, a time to mourn and a time to dance.

The verses in Ecclesiastes 3 are full of seasons, of moments, of highs and lows. They are a reminder to us that there is a time for everything, whether they are good times or bad times, we will encounter them all.

For me there has been many moments of joy, and equally many moments of pain. Over the years they have become meshed, and some of the things that brought me pain at the time have become incredible memorial stones I can now look back on and see the hand of God. I can see the way He has held me, how He stretched my faith, and led me through valleys and up onto mountain tops. I know that the things that were sent to destroy me have become some of my greatest stories of victory.

We serve a God who is the same yesterday, today and tomorrow. He knows where we've come from, and He knows where we are going. He sees the pitfalls before us, He sees the things that will hurt us and the things that will try to hold us down. But He also sees the beauty from ashes, He can see all the good that will come from the things that challenge us, and He walks with us through the times where our tears outnumber our smiles.

I know God has been with me in my greatest moments, the day I got married, when each of my children were born, when my books have been published, when I've encouraged others through the words I have written or spoken. But He has also been with me in the moments of heartbreak, when others have caused me pain beyond anything I thought possible, when I've had medical diagnosis's that I wasn't expecting, when life hasn't been what I thought it would be.

God is still God regardless of the weeping, or the laughing, whether we are mourning or dancing. He is still our greatest strength and our strongest refuge.

No matter what you might be facing right now, or where your journey might be taking you, lean into Him, and let Him be with you through every moment of your life.

Prayer

Lord Jesus, I thank you that in every moment you are with me. I am so grateful that I don't face each morning alone, I don't wake up in fear or dread, for I know you go before me into every circumstance.

Lord, as I look back over my life, I can see you in every situation, I see you when I've cried alone, and I see you when I've rejoiced with others. There has never been a time when I have felt like I have not been surrounded by your love. I know that you encircle me, you hem me in on every side and I am protected, cared for and loved.

Father God, I thank you that you are the giver of joy, you cause me to laugh and to experience such depths of happiness, and for this I am so grateful. But I know that you too allow sadness and tears to also be a part of our experience, that in every season we will face ups and downs, however, we don't face them alone.

Lord, in all things, you are my strength, you walk with me through the valleys and the mountains, on the days when I lose my way and it all becomes too hard, I know that it's in that place that you will carry me.

Amen.

Who Does God Say You Are?

1 Samuel 16:11 (MSG)

Then he asked Jesse "Is this it? Are there no more sons?"
"Well, yes, there's the runt. But he's out tending the sheep."
Samuel orders Jesse, "Go get him. We're not
moving from this spot until he's here."

W e are not defined by the words or thoughts of others, but only by God.

We see in this story that Samuel has been sent on a mission from God to find a king to replace Saul. He undertakes quite a journey as God leads him to the house of Jesse, who has many sons that are incredibly good prospects. Jesse parades around seven of these sons in front of Samuel, however, God rejects them all. So, Samuel asks Jesse if there are any others, and the words of Jesse are surprising to say the least. He does have one more son, but describes him as the runt, the youngest, the one who is out tending the sheep.

Jesse doesn't even call his son by name, but rather he describes him by his stature, and his position. And it is this son, David, who God chooses, and anoints as king.

So often we let others define who we are. We let our circumstances, our jobs, our place in society, and sometimes even the thoughts we have about ourselves, speak louder than the voice of God.

When God calls us into something, He isn't interested in what other people think of us, He doesn't care what our past looks like, or whether we are qualified. God looks at our hearts, and in His eyes, this is what defines us.

David was a shepherd boy, he was the youngest in his family, he was small, and even in the eyes of his father he was never going to be like his brothers. Yet, God chose David to be greater than them all, He chose David to rise, defeat a giant, and become a king.

Don't let others determine your future or the outcome for your life, that's God's job. Place everything in His hands and let Him lead you into your calling. It is God, not others, that will have the final say in who you are, what you do, and where you go.

Prayer

Father God, I thank you that when the world sees nothing in me, you see something great. You aren't looking at my credentials, my schooling or training, but rather you are looking at my heart. You see my willingness to follow you, to dedicate myself to your calling, and to set my heart on that which has purpose for you.

Lord, help me not to be fixated on trying to be what others want me to be, but rather help me to chase after what you want me to be. Give me a heavenly desire over a worldly one, let my passion be led by you, and help me to keep that as my focus.

God, when I look at others, may I see them through your eyes, rather than looking down on them. May I see all the incredible qualities you have placed in them. When they don't quite measure up to my standard, remind me that I don't always measure up either, but you choose to love me anyway.

Lord, help me to walk in tune with you, seeing myself and others only through your lens of love.

Amen.

Our Good Father

t is such a blessing to us that we have God as our Heavenly Father.

I know for some, it can be difficult to associate God as a good Father, when we may not have had a great experience with our earthly dad growing up. It can be hard to relate that a Heavenly Father can be very different to what we had in the natural.

Although I do have a wonderful relationship with my dad, I like to think of God as my grandfather. Someone who is older, and full of wisdom, someone who has time to just sit and listen, someone who is happy to journey through life with me and gives me sound advice.

The voice of God, spoken with the loving kindness of a grandfather is gentle and healing, it's a hug when life is hard, it's warmth on a cold day, and it's the soothing balm on an open wound.

There is just something so very special about having a relationship with someone who loves you without reason, who is for you in every situation, and who will fight for you when everyone else has walked away.

God in His loving kindness desires to be involved in every aspect of our lives, He chooses to love us on both our good and our bad days, He forgets all our failures and He forgives all our wrong doings.

He is the ultimate good Father, the most loyal and trustworthy friend.

Regardless of whether you think of God as your Father, or as your grandfather, just remember that to Him you are His most precious child, the one He would do anything for, and the one that He would travel to the ends of the earth to save.

I encourage you today to lean into Him, spend time in His presence, and walk in His ways. But mostly, remember how very much you are loved.

Prayer

Lord, I am so grateful that you are my Father, my confidant, my hiding place, my shield, and my forever friend.

I know without a shadow of a doubt that you love me with a love like no other. That in your eyes I am beautiful, I am the stars and the sun, and everything in-between.

I can barely fathom the blessing you poured out on me when you chose me as your own. When you created me, and then called me by name. You handpicked me and declared your great love for me.

Father God, I thank you that you are good, that your kindness surpasses anything I could have ever dreamed of, that you find little ways each day to express your unfathomable love for me.

You are Holy, wise and true, you are Majestic and all power-ful, you are above all things, and all things were set in motion because of you. Lord, you stepped down from Heaven to give yourself as a sacrifice for me, for no other reason except love.

My Father, I can never thank you enough, you are my Lord of all.

Amen.

The Great Commission

Matthew 28:19 (AMP)

Go therefore and make disciples of all the nations (help the people to learn of Me, believe in Me, and obey My words), baptising them in the name of the Father and of the Son and of the Holy Spirit.

The Great Commission, the words of Jesus, the commandment to us all.

We have been instructed to GO.

Go where you may ask?

We are to go into all the world, to anywhere and everywhere that needs to know the love of Jesus, to help others learn about Him, to encourage their belief in Him, and to teach them how to obey Him.

For you, all the world could be your own neighbourhood, your workplace, your school, or even your sporting club. For others it may be Africa, India, Asia or remote villages in South America. The 'where' isn't the sticking point, it's the 'going'. It's embarking on a journey that will bring Jesus to the world around you.

So often, we take our light and hide it under a bushel, rather than shining it for all to see. We hide our faith; we dim our passion, and we stay put in our comfort zone. We let obstacles keep us stuck, we get caught up in the here and now, we find it easier to stay in a place of 'waiting', and we think that the call to go is for someone else, not for us.

Jesus hasn't called us to be comfortable, He hasn't told us to plant our feet and be shackled by the treasures we have built up for ourselves. But rather He tells us to go and make disciples of all nations, to take the hope that we have inside of us and share it with a world that is lost and helpless.

He wants us to take up the challenge to make a difference, to have an eternal perspective, to pray for the world around us, and to live a life that is anchored and built in Him.

Today I would encourage you, wherever you are, get out of your comfort zone and GO make disciples of the world around you. Share your faith and shine for Jesus.

Prayer

Lord Jesus, help me to be obedient to your Word, help me to walk the path you have called me on, regardless of the outcome. Give me an eternal perspective, one that seeks out others and shares with them the truth of who you are.

Father, I thank you for open doors and opportunities, thank you that I can go where some others can't, and that through me the lost can find you. Lord, help me to remember that you have given me your words to carry, and that you will provide for me when the timing is right, to be your hands and feet.

Lord, fill me with courage, that I won't be held back, but I would stand up and speak your truth wherever I go. Remind me that I too was a sinner saved by grace, and it was by the courage of others speaking up that I came to know you. Help me to be that person for those around me.

Lord, wherever my feet may wander, bring others across my path who need your hope, your touch, and your love. Give me the willingness to go into all the world, to not become complacent, or so caught up in my own life that I refuse to reach out to others.

Jesus, I pray that my heart is in the right place with you, that I would continue to seek to do your will, and that I would be always prepared for all that you call me to.

Amen.

Are You Known By Your Fruit?

Matthew 7:16 (NLT)
You can identify them by their fruit, that is by the way they act.

This is such a challenging scripture, knowing that we will be identified by our fruit, by the way we act. When others see us, they will make a judgement call as to what sort of Christians we are, based on our behaviour and our attitude.

It's not enough to say that we are Christians, we need to BE Christians. We are to be an example of light in a world that is dark. We are to be the hands and feet of Jesus, doing good wherever we go.

The fruits of the spirit that we need to exhibit include love, joy, peace, kindness and goodness. It should be our desire that others notice these things in us. They need to see in us all that they would expect to see in God.

When we stay close to Jesus, grafted to the vine, we are continually being fed and renewed. Our spirit is being refreshed and we are receiving all the nutrients we need to flourish. However, when we choose to journey alone, when we try to take control of our lives, and when we think we know best, it's then that we stumble and fall.

We have been called to be followers of Jesus, to walk in His ways, to go into the world as His disciples, and do the things He did. As a Christian, living like Jesus is not an option, but rather it's a way of life. We have been given all the tools we need to share our faith, but by far the best thing we can do is to outwardly be a Godly example to those around us.

As you think on this today, take some time to reflect on which fruits require work to encourage growth, think on whether you are planted in good soil, and consider if you are staying grafted to the vine. Remember, good fruit will only flourish when well cared for, so let Jesus be the one who feeds and renews you today.

Prayer

Lord Jesus, when others look at me may they always see you. May I be a beautiful reflection of all that you are, a shining light in the dark, and a vessel of love in a loveless world.

Lord, help me to stay close to you, grafted to the vine, so that I might grow to be strong and productive, always being fruitful in season.

Father, help me to show the world what Christianity looks like, what it means to be a true follower of Christ. Help me to exhibit the fruits of the spirit, to endeavour to show love, joy, peace, patience, kindness, goodness, faithfulness, gentleness and self-control.

May I always act in a way that is worthy of the name of Jesus, that others would know from my actions who and what I am. Lord may they see less of me and more of you.

Lord, grow me in all the areas that need improvement, prune me and bring me into a place where I can flourish for you. I pray that I wouldn't be held back by the weeds of life, but that I would be refreshed and beautifully renewed.

Amen.

I Am

Exodus 3:14 (GNT)
God said "I AM WHO I AM."

There is such power in this.

God doesn't say I was, or I could be, or I might be, but He says I AM.

Those words come with promise, with hope, with strength and with encouragement.

He's not a God of the here today and gone tomorrow, but He is our constant. He is the one who is in the midst of every situation and circumstance. He is the One who was at the beginning and will remain until the end, He created the heavens and the earth, He is Lord overall. There is none like Him, there has never been any King, Saviour, or God that is even remotely like the Great I AM. He is all powerful, all knowing, and our all-loving Redeemer. He is full of grace and mercy, He is the forgiver of all, and the greatest love to all mankind. There is no need to doubt who He is, for He truly is who He says He is:

When you feel overwhelmed, He says I AM with you.

When you feel disappointed, He says I AM holding you.

When you can't face tomorrow, He says I AM going before you.

When you are waiting on healing, He says I AM the God who heals.

There is no place that you can go that God does not go with you, there is no valley too low, or mountain too high. Wherever you journey, He is there too.

He says, I AM your peace in the storm.

I AM your water in the desert.

I AM your victory in the hard place.

I AM your strength in times of need.

God is not too small to be all that you need, He is who He says He is, and He will do all that He says He will do.

Today I would encourage you not to be limited by who you think God is, but be blown away by the truth of who He tells you He is, and that is, He is the great I AM.

Prayer

Lord, I thank you for who you are, I thank you that in every circumstance, you are Lord of all.

Father, when my doubt tries to overwhelm me, when fear takes over, and when the world tries to convince me that I'm all alone, I thank you that your presence shines through. I thank you that you remind me of who I am, and of how much you love me.

Heavenly Father, I am so grateful that I can trust in you, that you go before me, and you surround me on all sides. I need not fear the terror of night, for you are my protector.

Lord Jesus, I thank you that you are my healer, my provider, my victory, and my peace in the storm.

Father God, I can rest in full assurance knowing that you will always be my constant, when others walk away, you will stay by my side. I will never have to fear that your love for me is fickle, for you will continue to hold onto me when others let go.

In all things, and through all things, Lord Jesus you truly are the great I AM.

Amen.

Be Set Apart

1 Kings 18:21 (GNT)
Elijah went up to the people and said, "How much longer will it take
you to make up your minds? If the Lord is God, worship him; but
if Baal is God, worship him!" But the people didn't say a word.

The world we live in is very much about living for today, about doing what makes us feel good, or makes us happy. We don't want to be too committed to one thing or another, in case a better option comes along.

Unfortunately, this is also how a lot of people walk out their faith. In their journey with God, they sit on the fence between practising Christianity and being like all of those around them. But God hasn't called us to be the same as the world, rather He calls us to be set apart.

We are not to be of the world, but to be the light that shines in the world. We are to be the 'better option'.

We read in Luke 11:23 the words of Jesus who says, 'He who is not with me is against me...'. Is that what we want? Is this how we want Jesus to perceive us, as someone who is against Him?

We can't afford to be fickle in our decision making about whether we are with Jesus or we're not. It isn't like going between football teams, cheering on the one who happens to be winning this week, and basing our decisions on what happens to suit us on the day.

A Christ filled life is one where we choose God every day. It's not a matter of giving Him our best today, but tomorrow might be a different story, depending on who we are with or what we are doing. As the scripture says, 'If we are not for Him, then we are against Him'. It's one way or the other.

On the day of judgement, we want to be all in, we want Him to remember us, to know us by the way we lived, by the choices we made, and by the decision to be 100% for Him.

I would encourage you today to choose your steps carefully, to not sit on the fence, but to be wholly dedicated in your service of the one and only living God.

Prayer

Lord Jesus, I thank you that you are the light of the world, that you shine in dark places and bring hope to all those who trust in you.

Father, help me to keep my eyes fixed on you, to choose you in all circumstances, and to remember that it is you, and only you, who is to be praised.

God, on the days when I feel lost, when I am apathetic, and when I go back and forth in my decision making, remind me that when I choose you, I am choosing life, hope and truth.

Lord, let me live my best life for you, holding nothing back, but giving you all I am in order that my days would go well. When I am torn between what I know is right, and what the world is calling out to me, help me to always stand my ground, to fix my gaze and to be wholly sold out for you.

Jesus, you are my beginning and end, the reason I get up each day, and my purpose in all I do. May I always hold fast to the love I have for you, and may I never be found to be sitting on the fence, but rather, I would be found in the house of the Lord forever.

Amen.

Run Your Race

1 Corinthians 9:24 (NIV)
Do you not know that in a race all the runners run, but only
one gets the prize? Run in such a way as to get the prize.

Several years ago, I decided to take up running, I thought it would be a great way to get fit and shed some kilos. What I hadn't counted on was how hard it would be. I am not a natural runner; I find it hard to run and breathe at the same time. I am also slightly uncoordinated and lack the ability to plough through the pain barrier, whilst not falling over my own feet.

I have watched many athletes make running look easy, I have seen them glide along almost as if they are running on air. I've seen them stand on podiums and receive their prizes for winning the race that they have run. I know the discipline that it would have taken for them to get to this point, the journey they would have embarked on that meant gruelling hours on a treadmill or hitting the pavement day after day.

It is similar with our Christian life; we are encouraged to run in such a way as to receive the prize. This means we need to put in the hard yards, we need to train our minds, our hearts and our bodies to excel in all that we do. We need to commit to the task at hand, setting aside all else to run the race that God has called us to.

The Christian journey is not always easy, it's not necessarily a straight path or flat ground. There can be many twists and turns, there can be mountains that need to be climbed, and valleys that need to be navigated. The way of success through all of this is discipline, its training, it's being100% sold out for the cause. It is not for the feint hearted or those who give up or give in easily, but the prize is worth fighting for.

I would encourage you today to run your race with passion, put aside all else and do not give up. Get up early and spend time preparing, know the race that you have been called to, and train for it with diligence.

This is the way to receive your prize.

Prayer

Lord, I thank you that you have called me to journey with you, to enter the race with my eyes fixed firmly on the prize, and to be steadfast in my dedication and endurance.

God, on the days when I want to give up, when I am distracted, and when I don't feel like I can keep going, remind me of my calling, of my hope in you, and of my need to persevere.

Father, I pray that you would open the eyes of my heart that I might be wholly sold out for you, that I would stand my ground, fix my gaze, and run with earnest desire and passion towards the prize, and that prize is you.

Give me clear vision and insight, not being easily swayed by the crowd, not moved by all that is going on around me, but rather help me to navigate the mountain and the valley knowing that you go before me.

Lord, on my best days and on my worst days, be my first and not my last. Remind me to call out to you, to hold tight to you, and to trust you in every storm.

And on my final day, when I stand on the podium, Lord may I hear your voice say, 'Well done my good and faithful servant'.

Amen.

Follow God's Instructions

Genesis 7:5 (NIV)
And Noah did all that the Lord commanded him.

We all know the story of Noah, how God told him to build an ark for his family and the animals, for the world was going to be destroyed by a flood, but all those in the ark would be saved.

In what seemed like crazy circumstances, Noah did all that God asked him to do, and he and his family, along with the animals, lived, whilst the rest of the earth was destroyed.

Sometimes we are faced with circumstances in our lives that seem crazy, they seem completely left of field, and we are given the choice to trust God and follow Him in what appears to be a hopeless situation or go our own way.

Noah could have laughed in the face of God's instructions. He could have turned his back and thought to himself 'That will never happen'. There had never been torrential rain before, yet God was saying that a flood was coming, and that he needed to build a boat.

Surely not?

But Noah was a man who believed in God, who trusted in Him, who had embarked on a journey with Him and who had great faith in Him. If God said it would happen, then it would. If God asked him to build a boat, then that is what he would do.

How often has God instructed us in the way we should go and yet we deliberate on what to do? We sit, we think, we ponder, we agonise, we seek counsel, and we go back and forth on whether to follow His instructions or not.

There are times we take things into our own hands, we think we must have heard God wrong, we come up with excuses why we can't do what He has asked.

There are times when we think we know better than God. We rationalise the things He has asked us to do, the doors He asks us to walk through, or the doors He asks us to close. We determine in our hearts that surely God would never ask us to walk away from people, or situations, or jobs, or lifestyles that we enjoy, to live closer to Him.

Today I would encourage you to be like Noah, to hear the voice of God, and to follow Him in all your ways.

Prayer

Father God, I know that your ways are always best, that you have only my best interests at heart, and that you desire to walk with me each step of the way, every day.

Lord, help me to keep my heart toward you, to stay in tune with your Holy Spirit, to be listening for your voice, and then to follow your commands.

God, help me to let go of control, help me to lay down all my thoughts, my hopes, my pre-conceived ideas, to live a life worthy of you.

God, may I have the spirit of Noah within me, one that not only hears from you, but follows you regardless of the cost. Give me a spirit filled perspective that I might look up rather than down, following you rather than after worldly value.

Lord, may I always put my trust in you, knowing that you can see all things, and that you ultimately know what is the best path for me to follow, Help me to rely on you when in the natural I would choose to rely only on myself, and Lord help me to rest in you, when the days are hard and I've somehow lost my way.

Thank you, God, that you are my ark in the storm.

Amen.

You Are Known

Psalm 139:1 (ICB)
Lord, you have examined me, you know all about me.

S adly, the world we live in is a place where lying is the norm, it's not something that is just done on occasion, but it is has become habitual and is seen as almost an acceptable thing to do. We laugh when others tell highly exaggerated stories, knowing full well that the amount of truth in them is minimal, yet we don't call others out, as it's all just a bit of fun.

Quite often we lie to ourselves, we pretend it doesn't hurt when others are chosen over us, when we are overlooked or forgotten. We lie about how we feel when we aren't acknowledged or seen, we push down our emotions and put on a brave face, not just for others, but also for ourselves.

But there is One we can never lie to, we may try, but He sees straight through our lies, and into the depths of who we really are. God knows us, He knows everything about us, every thought we have, long before we even think it. Before that tear slides down your cheek, God knows it's coming. We may try to pretend everything is ok, but who do we think we're fooling? God isn't like our friends or our family, He can't be hoodwinked, we can't pull the wool over His eyes. He can see into the depths of our hearts, and He knows exactly what is going on.

We may let others believe that all is well in our lives, even when we're falling apart, but we can't tell God the same lie and expect Him to believe it, because He knows us, and He can see the truth. He has journeyed with us through many hardships, so before we say a word, He knows what we're going to say, before we try to run, He knows where we're planning on going. He was the One who formed us and shaped us, so why would we think we can lie to the One who knows us so intimately, and not be found out?

Today, I would encourage you to have an honest conversation with God, share your heart with Him, let Him know your greatest hurts and fears, and trust that for you, He will be more than enough.

Prayer

Father God, I thank you that you created me in your image, that before I was even a twinkling in my parent's eyes, I was a daughter of yours.

Lord, forgive me for all the times I have held back from you, the times when I have tried to hide who I am, when I have retreated into a shell and pretended everything was ok, when really, I was falling apart.

Dear Jesus, I need you more than ever, I need you to hold me on the days when I can no longer stand, I need you to walk with me and to give me the courage to keep going when it would be easier to just stop. I need you to remind me of who I am, and mostly I need to know that you will never leave me, even when I am at my worst.

Father, you can see into my heart, you know my deepest hurts, the wounds that I keep hidden. You can see what I hide from the world around me, the pain, the sorrow, the grief, the anguish and the torment. Only you can see the real me. I pray for your healing hand over every area of my life.

Holy Spirit, fill me with your peace that I might know that I am held, not in the arms of judgement, but in the arms of love. That I would know that my Father is caring for me, and that I can share my heart with honesty and truth, knowing that I am His and He is mine.

Amen.

Be Determined

Deuteronomy 31:6 (GNT)
Be determined and confident. Do not be afraid of them. Your God, the
LORD himself, will be with you. He will not fail or abandon you.

This is such a powerful promise to us. It speaks of strength, of hope and of victory.

We have no need to be afraid or fearful, for God is with us, He will never fail us, nor abandon us.

The dictionary describes the word determined as 'having made a firm decision and being resolved not to change it'. This determination is the faith we have in God, we are determined to trust in Him, to place our faith in His truth and His promises. We can stand firm on who He is, knowing that His character never changes, so He is our safe place.

We can be full of confidence, or courage, knowing that He is taking care of us, and we will never be alone. We can be wholly dependent on the One who was at the beginning and will be at the end. We can rely fully on the One who walks with us on our journey through life.

At any given moment we can be subject to fear, to crumble in the face of adversity, to lose all hope. Yet, God continues to walk with us, to uphold us, to keep providing for us, and to weather the storms with us. He has given us His assurance and has reminded us of the fact that He is sovereign.

Each of us have had moments of being overwhelmed, by our situations, by the news reports, by the onslaught of disappointment, yet God in His faithfulness has continued to be our peace in the storm.

Today I would encourage you remain determined, steadfast and firm in your faith. To be confident in our God, the one who is the same yesterday, today and forever.

Let Him be your truth, knowing that He will continue to walk with you, never failing or abandoning you. He is your strength and your courage, hold onto that today.

Prayer

Lord, today I choose to put my hope, my trust, and my faith in you. When the world tries to test me, and the very ground I stand on begins to shake, I will determine in my heart that I will continue to be steadfast and follow you.

God, fill me with the strength that I need to stand firm, to not look to the left or the right, but rather to stay focused on you, my shelter and safe place.

Father, help me in my unbelief, in my doubt, my fear, and my resolve. Give me the ability to walk with my head held high and an attitude that is positive and strong. Keep me in your perfect peace as I travel through the unknown and face all that would try to destroy me.

Help me to be confident and courageous as I step out in my faith, and always remind me that my dependence is on you, not on myself. When I find my heart quickening and fear settling in, help me to realign myself with you and to come back under the shadow of your Holy Spirit.

God, I thank you for your provision, that I can trust in you rather than in myself or in others. I thank you that I need not be overwhelmed, or filled with disappointment, but rather I can be at rest, knowing that you will never fail me nor abandon me, for you will be with me wherever I go.

Amen.

Getting Along With Others

Psalm 133:1 (MSG)
How wonderful, how beautiful, when brothers and sisters get along

From the beginning of time, there has been anarchy amongst family, amongst friends and within the church.

There have been quarrels between siblings vying for the love of their parents, between the disciples over which one of them was the greatest, and between religious groups as to who was right in their theological views.

However, this kind of behaviour, and this attitude, was never what God intended.

In the garden of Eden, He created man, He then went on to create a helper for him so that he wouldn't have to do life alone. Yet from there, we have seen a heavy decline in what God intended, and the life we are living.

In recent times we have seen war break out across the world, and the ramifications of this are long lasting, and stretch far and wide.

Jesus has told us to 'Love each other just as I have loved you'.

He didn't say to love each other if things were going well, for as long as you feel like it, or as long as you're getting your own way, but to love the way that He does.

The love of Jesus was sacrificial, it was the laying down of His life for ours, it was the kind of love that overlooks wrongs, and that forgives faults. This is the love He wants us to have for each other. He wants us to put others first, to put aside our own wants and needs and to share all that we have with those around us. Jesus wants us to pour our hearts into the broken, the lost, the unlovable, and the unwanted, it is in doing this that we become more like Him.

As you journey through your week, look for opportunities to spend time with others, focus on the positives and don't get bogged down with the negativities. Let go of hurts and find ways to connect with those you may have previously dismissed as being too hard to get along with. In doing this we are loving others in the way God intended. This is the beginning of walking together in unity, which has always been God's plan for His people.

Prayer

Lord, I thank you that you created each of us in your image, and that you love us with a love that surpasses all understanding. That your love knows no bounds, and that we are held tightly within the security of your arms.

God, I pray that this week you would show me how to love others on a deeper level. That I would grasp the depth of care you have for those around me. Teach me to see past the face, the clothes, the background, and the abilities of all those I encounter and let me see into their hearts to see who they truly are.

Lord Jesus, forgive me for all the times that I have been nit-picky, for my judgemental attitude, and for my short sightedness when it comes to those in my world, I ask now that you fill my heart with love and compassion towards those in my family, my workplace, and my community.

God, I pray for unity, for respect of each other's opinions and beliefs. I pray that my heart would be pure before you and that you would help me be the one who reaches out in love to others, as a way of honouring you, and blessing them.

Amen.

Make A Joyful Noise

Psalm 95:1 (NIV)
Come, let us sing for joy to the Lord, let us shout
aloud to the Rock of our salvation.

We have all been to concerts and shows where we have sung along, clapped our hands, jumped up and down, danced and made a whole lot of noise. We've taken trips and gone on journeys to see our favourite popstars perform at incredible arenas. We've revered the singer or the group, praising them for their talent and have followed them on social media to stay abreast of all that they do.

And yet, they are only people, and as wonderful as their music may be, it can be here today and gone tomorrow. Of course, there are those whose music spans many generations, who truly are icons in their field, and have certainly given us reason to keep going back for more.

But this got me to thinking…. what about God?

Do we sing, and dance, and shout aloud for His glory? Do we jump up and down and make a lot of noise in honour of Him? Do we take the time to journey to places where we can see His creation, or to hear others speak about the great things He is doing?

Surely, He is worthy of our following, our reverence, and our praise?

God is the ultimate in all things, He is the music, the song, and the very reason for all that we do and all that we are. God is our purpose and our passion, He is our heart and our soul, and therefore deserves His rightful place within us.

It seems we feel comfortable standing in a crowded auditorium chanting along to the beat of somebody else's drum, yet how often when it comes to worshipping God, we suddenly become withering wall flowers, not wanting to step out of our comfort zone to raise our hands and shout a hallelujah.

Today I would encourage you to sing, to shout, to dance, and to give God your all. Let Him know that He is Lord, and that you put Him above all else.

Along with the angels, may you be found to be singing 'Holy Holy Holy to the Lord God Almighty, who was, and is, and is to come.'

Prayer

Lord, I ask your forgiveness for all the times I've honoured others over you, for the times when I've given praise to singers, or actors, and yet not given you the praise you deserve.

Jesus, I pray that you would give me a heart that is set on you, that is ready to worship you at any time, ready to sing in adoration, and ready to lift up my hands to glorify your name.

God, you alone are worthy, for it is you, and only you, who put the stars and the sun in the sky, who separated the east from the west, and who brought all of creation into being. Let me never forget who it is that is above all, who it is that is worthy of all praise.

Father, as I step out into today, may I see your handiwork all around me, and may I once again be in awe of the beauty you have provided for us. In the wind, the trees, the mountains, the raindrops, and the sunset, may I see you everywhere I go.

Lord, I thank you for all you have made, and I give you your rightful place as Lord, God of the universe, and holder of all.

Amen

Summer And Winter

Psalm 104:19 (NLT)
You made the moon to mark the seasons, and the sun knows when to set.

Have you ever felt that you're in a holding pattern between seasons?

That you've moved out of one season, but haven't quite moved into the next?

Sometimes God will hold us in a place of rest, a place where we stop, where we take a break from the rush and just sit with Him.

There is something uncomfortable about the waiting, it's hard to be doing nothing when we want to move full steam ahead. It's not easy being in a holding pattern, just perched on the edge of moving into the next big thing. We find it hard to envision that part of our journey requires that we just stop, and for a time, do nothing.

However, God promises us there is a purpose in His timing, in His season for us, and we just need to learn the art of waiting on Him. Sometimes we wait because there are lessons to be learnt, sometimes because we will become burnt out if we don't stop, and there are times when God determines that we are just not ready for what lies ahead.

Seasons are beautiful, they reflect God's love, they are His smile on a sunny day, and His tears with us in the cold of winter. Each change of season brings with it the opportunity of a new beginning, a brand-new day, and the hope of what is still to be birthed in us. We don't always see seasons the same way God does, so maybe it's time to ask Him to give us a new perspective.

God leads us from one day and into the next, but in the space between, there in the dark of night. It is in this place that He holds us in His arms, in a place of rest, a place of waiting.

Today, if you feel left behind, if you feel like God hasn't moved fast enough, that He hasn't heard your prayer or your cry, remember that He is with you in the waiting. Just because you have moved out of one season and you don't seem to be in the thick of the next, trust God in the waiting.

Know that He has a plan and a purpose to every season under heaven.

Prayer

Father, I thank you that in every season of life you are with me. During the warmth of summer, and into the frosty nights of winter, you remain steadfast.

Help me Lord to trust you in the waiting, to know that you have my best interests at heart and that I sometimes need to just stop and hold tight until you give me the go ahead to continue moving forward.

Lord, when I am uncomfortable, when I want to step out, when I find myself pacing the floor, and when I have trouble with the quiet of each day, remind me that you have a purpose for me, in what seems like the end.

God, help me to know the difference between when you say 'no' and when you say 'wait'. Remind me that all you do is for my good, and that you see what lies ahead and whether it will benefit me or cause me to be distressed.

As I move from one season to the next, help me to remain focused on you and not be swept away by the little things. Help me as I find my way and stumble through new beginnings, and Father God I pray, be with me each step of the way.

Amen.

Refuse To Worry

Matthew 6:34 (TPT)
Refuse to worry about tomorrow, but deal with each challenge that
comes your way, one day at a time. Tomorrow will take care of itself.

By nature, I tend to be a worrier, an overthinker, and an active planner.

I like to have a plan for every situation, and not just one plan, but I need a backup plan in case things don't go the way I had hoped or thought they would.

Does any of this sound familiar to you? Do you have the need to be in control of all that is happening? So much so that you lie in bed at night coming up with contingencies for all the things that haven't happened yet?

God, in His wisdom, knew that at some point in our journey we would all worry, we would all be filled with anxiety or fear, and He says throughout the bible, 365 times to be exact, for us not to worry. Yet we still do.

I love the Passion translation of this verse in Matthew, it tells us to 'refuse to worry about tomorrow', which completely acknowledges that we will in fact be thinking about what tomorrow holds, but we need to stay strong, be vigilant, hold tight, and be determined in our refusal to let the worries of tomorrow come upon us today.

Tomorrow's challenge is not today's problem, so there's no need to start panicking about it or planning for it already, but rather, we deal with it when it happens. Enjoy the journey, don't just rush to the destination.

For some, living in the moment can be difficult, taking one day at a time can be a skill that requires practise. We are not all wired to just take each day as it comes, but rather we are planning weeks, months, and years in advance. There are times when we think that once this or that happens our lives will be different, things will get better. We think it's once we meet our partner, or when we get a new job, or when our kids grow up, or when this situation passes. We have our lives on hold waiting for a new and better tomorrow.

Considering this, I would encourage you to take one day at time, hand over your tomorrow to God and let Him deal with that, but for now, just live and love in the moment.

Prayer

Lord, you know me so well, you know when I sit down and when I rise up, you know every thought that enters my mind, you know the beats of my heart and the cries from the depths of my soul. There is nothing of me that is hidden from you.

You can see each one of my needs, you know my greatest fears, and you see me as I sit and worry for all that may or may not be ahead.

God, I pray that you help me to release all control to you, that as I find myself facing fear over what tomorrow may hold, that you would help me to open my hands and let you take everything that I am clinging to so tightly.

Lord Jesus, help me not to overthink every situation, but to trust that you have it all in hand. Give me the strength to 'refuse to worry', to stand my ground, and to know that I can rest assured in the knowledge that you are the holder of tomorrow, not me.

Father, you know that I struggle to be still, that I make plans upon plans, and that I like to be in control of everything around me. Lord, I pray that you would remove this burden from me and help me to just place my trust in you, and in doing so, take one day at a time.

God, you created the universe, you lit up the sky and filled the sea, help me to remember all of this when I worry if you can take care of all that I hold onto. Remind me that you, not me, are the giver of life.

Amen.

Friends Refresh The Soul

Proverbs 27:9 (MSG)
Just as lotions and fragrance give sensual delight,
a sweet friendship refreshes the soul.

There is nothing more refreshing than the time spent in the company of good friends, the time spent laughing, reminiscing, and enjoying the moments that you have together.

For those of us who have been blessed with precious friendships, we know the joy that is found in sharing our journey, knowing we are cared about, having others pray for us, and praying for them in return.

But there can be times in all friendships when there is a longing for things to be different, for wishing our lives looked more like theirs, or for that feeling of being left behind when others are experiencing joys that we too wish we could have. We may be desiring more money, marriage, children or grandchildren, we may wish our lives were entirely different to what they are..

This doesn't mean that there is a problem with our friendships, it just means that we have unmet needs or wants in our lives. It doesn't mean that we wish our friends weren't experiencing blessing, but rather that we may feel disappointed that we are in a different season.

God created friendship, He knew that each of us would have needs in our hearts, our minds and our beings that could only be met by others. He knew that we would desire to make connections with those who are like-minded to us, those who make us laugh, or share our vision, or are walking the same journey as us.

Our souls long for refreshment, they desire the sweetness that is fulfilled by friendship, as we crave to stand beside others and feel like we belong.

Proverbs 17:17 says 'A friend loves at all times…'. All times, not just when things are going well, not just when we are in the same season, not just when it suits, but all times.

Let today be the day that you love those God has placed in your tribe, that you refresh those who are part of your village. Get alongside the lonely and show them support and care, carve out opportunities for friendship with those you stand beside.

Be the friend that God has called you to be.

Prayer

Lord Jesus, I thank you for those you have placed in my life, I thank you for the journey we are taking together, not necessarily all going to the same place at the same time, but all standing as one through it all.

Lord, you have blessed me with the most incredible friends, those who fill my cup daily. Help me never to take these friendships for granted, but to treasure them, and continue to grow them through every season of life. Give me opportunities to lavish my friends with love, to hold them up with prayer, and to stand beside them when the circumstances of life become hard.

Father, I pray that you would help me to offer grace, to freely forgive, and to be willing to turn the other cheek when hurts come my way. Remind me that even the best of friends can wound us, as you yourself were wounded by those you loved. On the days when I feel let down and discarded, help me to remain loyal and kind.

God, help me to celebrate the highs and be empathetic during the lows, not just a friend who is around for the good times, but one who 'sticks closer than a brother' when things get tough. Give me the words to say when I am at a loss and show me what it takes to love like you.

Lord, you are the greatest friend of all, let me learn from you. Amen.

Have Hope

Psalm 31:24 NIV
Be strong and take heart, all of you who hope in the Lord.

The keyword in this verse is 'hope'. All those who have their hope in the Lord can be strong and courageous.

Our hope is not in man, in governments, in medicine, or in science, our hope is in God. He is the one who will never let us down, He will never lie to us or deceive us, He will never abandon us when things get too tough, or when the way looks too hard.

God is with us in the good times and the bad. He is with us when the days are hard, when we don't know what to do, or how to move forward. No matter what situation we are facing, or where we are on our journey of faith, we can rest in the knowledge that He is with us, and He is the anchor for our soul. All we need to do is continue to hope in God, to continue to put our faith and trust in Him. He doesn't expect us to have all the answers, but He wants us to know that He does. He knows what the days ahead look like, He can see the exact path that you and I will travel on, and He promises to walk beside us every step of the way.

Therefore, we know that in trusting Him, in hoping in Him, we can be strong and courageous, we can face any storm that comes our way, or any mountain that stands before us. We will not be overwhelmed, nor will we be overcome, because God is our hope.

No matter what life throws at us, we can remain steadfast, we can hold a position of peace, knowing that we are watched over, protected, held and loved.

Today I would encourage you to stand with strength and courage, knowing that God goes before you in the battle. Be courageous, for He is with you always, you will never walk alone. Most importantly continue to put your hope and faith in God, for He is the one who has the answers, the one who knows beginning to end, and He is the one who surrounds you and holds you in safety and love.

Prayer

Father God, I thank you that my hope is in you, that I don't have to rely on my own strength, or put my faith in those around me, but rather I can hold onto you as my Saviour.

Lord, when the world tries to wear me down, when it bombards me with lies and deceptions, when I grow weary from trying to stand under the pressure of expectation, I pray that your peace would continue to surround me.

When the days seem hard, and I feel like I can't move forward, remind me that I don't have to walk in my own strength, but that you are the one holding me, guiding me and leading me.

Jesus, be my hope for tomorrow, my reason for getting up in the morning, be the song in my heart and the joy in my soul, let me never forget that you are the rising and the setting of all things, there is nothing too hard for you.

Lord, I ask that you give me courage, that I would step out boldly, living free from fear, knowing that you have my back, and I am forever held in the safety of your arms.

Amen.

Judge Not

Romans 14:10 (ICB)
So why do you judge your brother in Christ? And why
do you think that you are better than he is? We will
all stand before God, and he will judge us all.

recently had a conversation with someone where I said the words 'It wasn't the way I would have done it'.

As soon as I'd said it, I knew that my words implied that what had been done was less than perfect, it wasn't ideal, it wasn't up to my standards and therefore it wasn't as good as it could have been.

I gave the impression that my way would have been so much better, and although I never actually said that I certainly inferred it and had indirectly criticised what had been done.

There are many times in life when we judge the actions or behaviour of someone else. When we take what we see at face value, not really knowing the full picture, and we make a judgement call on it. We give our opinions, whether they are asked for or not, and in doing so we jump to conclusions and make assumptions based on what we think we may know, which may not necessarily be true.

In all the instances where Jesus could have judged or criticized, He only loved. He offered grace and mercy and forgiveness. He never looks at any of us and sees a sinner. He may see sin, but He doesn't define us by that, but rather He chooses to overlook that and love us anyway.

As followers of Jesus, we are called to imitate Him, to walk in His ways, to learn from Him and to take on His character. He wants us to be more like Him, which means loving others the way He loves them, not judging them, or criticising them, but seeing the best in them, just as He sees the best in us.

To be like Jesus requires sacrifice, it means dying to self, not finding fault in others but esteeming them higher than we do ourselves. It may mean changing our direction, walking a different journey or finding a better way.

Today I would encourage you to take on the traits of Jesus, love the way He does, and let the world see His light shining through you, bringing hope to a hopeless world.

Prayer

Father God, forgive me for all the times I have judged and criticised others, where I have looked down on their behaviour or their actions, and have thought myself better than them. Forgive me for thinking that I know better and that my ways are superior to those around me.

Lord, help me to love like you do, putting others first. Remind me of what it looks like to 'love my neighbour as myself', to care about the needs of others more than my own needs, and to always be willing to go the extra mile.

I pray that you fill my heart with kindness, grace and mercy. Let me never forget how you have overlooked all my downfalls, and therefore I too need to overlook those of others. Help me not to hold onto grudges, but to hand them to you, and then to move forward in love.

Jesus, in following your example, may I learn to die to self, may I imitate your ways, knowing that they are always best.

Father God, go before me in all I do, teach me your ways, and walk with me as I learn to live like you.

Amen.

Be Still

Exodus 14:14 (NIV)
The Lord will fight for you; you need only to be still.

We live in a world that has no idea how to be still. We struggle with the concept of not having a plan, of not knowing what is happening tomorrow or next week or even next year. We live by our diaries and planners, and we are constantly checking our available dates, usually to fill them with events that we 'can't possibly miss'.

We need to have all our ducks lined up in a row, we feel the need to have it all figured out, to have A, B and C sorted. We need a contingency ready 'just in case'. Our minds are constantly on the next big thing, we are always looking ahead at what is coming up and what we need to be prepared for.

Yet this is not the life God would have for us, He doesn't want our lives to be defined by our 'to do list', but rather, by waiting on Him, on seeking Him first, and by sitting in stillness hearing His voice. He has promised that He will go before us, He will fight for us, and all that is required of us is to be still.

Being still is not about jumping headfirst into every opportunity, it's not about 24/7 activities, it's not even about serving to capacity, but it's about letting go of all the things that need done, all the places you need to be and the people you need to see. It's about giving God time to speak into your life, to walk with you and to refresh you. It's allowing Him to go into battle for you when you can no longer keep fighting.

There are plenty of opportunities to fill our days with things to do, there will always be open doors to serve others, and without doubt there will always be another battle to fight, but sometimes we just need to stop, we need to wait, and we need to be still, knowing that God has us.

As we head into another busy day, as we move forward on our journey, remember to take time out, and just sit in the presence of God, allowing Him to be the one who fills your heart, your head, and your life.

Prayer

Lord, as I sit here in the quiet, help me to be fully present with you, not thinking ahead, not looking back, but wholly in your presence, in the place you have called me to be.

As my mind leads me to my tick list, my battle plans for the day or the week, help me to settle my thoughts and to bring them back into submission to you. Remind me that it is you who orders my steps, and that I only need to be still and wait for you to lead me forward.

Jesus, teach me the art of just being, not serving, not giving, not striving, not fighting and certainly not planning, but just being still. That I might find a time of peace and quiet, where my heart is simply held by you, and I am fully immersed in who you are.

Lord, redefine for me the art of stillness, show me the benefits of stopping, of sitting, of resting, and of clearing everything away. Let me not see this as a waste of time, but rather a time of gathering strength, finding peace, discovering courage, and gaining insight.

Jesus, as I seek to be more like you, remind me that you too needed to get away, be still, and renew your strength. So, as I learn to imitate you, let me also learn to just 'be still and know that you are God'.

Amen.

The Greatest Is Love

---

1 Corinthians 13:13 (NLT)
Three things will last forever – faith, hope, and
love – and the greatest of these is love.

I n recent years I have had the joy of watching my son get married, he committed himself forever to the love of his life. He stood beside the girl of his dreams and uttered the words "I do", joining himself into a sanctified partnership with the one he has chosen to share his life with.

Entering marriage is one of the biggest decisions that any individual will ever make, it involves giving and taking, dying to self, and thinking of another more highly than yourself.

Falling in love is something we do, staying in love is something we choose.

The Bible tells us that of all the things that last forever, love is the greatest, it is the single most important factor in life.

We read throughout scripture so many stories and hear so many commands about loving one another. We read about putting others before ourselves, about turning the other cheek, giving without expectation of receiving, and forgiving, even when it's hard.

In John 15:13 it says, 'Greater love has no one than this, to lay down one's life for one's friends.' What an incredible portrayal of love, the greatest sacrifice, to give up your own life for your friend, for the one you care about. To put aside your own desires, your wants, and needs, and allow another to become more important than yourself.

This too is an excellent description of how marriage looks, it is being willing to give up your dreams so that your spouse can follow theirs, it's saying no to what you may want to do with friends, or at work, so that you can spend quality time with your partner. It's all the small things that you let go of so that you can build on the one thing that really matters. It's a journey you take together, husband and wife, in partnership with God.

Today I encourage you, if God has blessed you with a marriage partner, love them the way we have been called to love, forsaking all others, and choosing them above all else.

Prayer

Father God, I thank you for the gift of marriage, for the blessing of having a best friend to stand with throughout the journey of life.

Lord, I thank you for giving me my person, for letting me share my daily ups and downs, my good days and bad days with the one you have chosen for me.

Jesus, bless them today, encourage them in all they do, lift them up when things seem hard, and help them to trust you with the big things as well as the small.

Lord, give me the attributes that I need to make my marriage flourish, help me to show love, kindness and forgiveness. Help me to turn the other cheek when needed, to go the extra mile, and to be faithful in all ways.

Lord, just as you chose Eve for Adam, I thank you that you have chosen the love of my life for me. Whilst I know there are days that are hard, days when I may be bruised, or days when everything goes wrong, help me to never forget that what you 'have joined together, no one can separate.'

Lord, I pray your continued blessing on my marriage, that we may walk together towards you, and that in all things, Father God, may you be glorified.

Amen.

Faith Hope Trust

Matthew 14:28-30 (NIV)
"Lord, if it's you," Peter replied, "tell me to come to you on the water."
"Come," He said. Then Peter got down out of the boat, walked on
the water, and came toward Jesus. But when he saw the wind, he
was afraid and, beginning to sink, cried out, "Lord, save me!"

What an incredible story of faith, of trust, and of God walking with those He loves during the hardest moments of life.

We see in this story that God doesn't always calm the storm before He asks us to step out in faith. He doesn't always change our circumstances before He asks us to change our attitude. Sometimes it's in the middle of the battle or during the tempest that He gives us opportunity to exercise our faith and move forward.

I am sure for all of us there have been times that we have waited for healing to come, for calm to be restored, or for people and situations to change. It's hard to trust God when we are overwhelmed, when all around us appears out of control, and when the easiest thing to do is just step back. Getting out of the boat is hard, it can be frightening, and it requires all the faith we can muster to trust that God will hold us.

But in all things, we know that we are not alone. Whilst the disciples were being tossed about by the raging sea, Jesus walked toward them. He didn't leave them cowering in fear, He never let their boat sink, or the sea take them captive, but on the hardest journey they had faced so far, He went to them. It is the same for each of us, we are not left alone to face our fears, but Jesus comes alongside us and reaches out to us, asking us to step out in faith and walk to Him.

I would encourage you today, that no matter what boat you are in, how far out to sea you feel, or how gripped by fear you may be, step out in faith and walk towards God. He will never let you fall, and His hand will always be outstretched towards you, calling you safely back towards Him.

Prayer

Lord Jesus, I thank you that you are my safe harbour, you are the place I call home and where I run to during the hard seasons of my life.

Thank you, God, that I can place my faith in you, that I don't need to face the stormy seas alone, for you are with me always. You are my rock and my shelter.

Lord, grow my faith that I might trust you more, that when I call out to you, I know you are never far off, but always by my side. Help me to lean on you when I don't understand what is happening, let my hope in you be without borders, so that I can stand firm on the days when my world is shaking.

Jesus, I am so grateful that you carry me when I can't walk any further, you hold me when my days are dark, and you whisper words of assurance when I am filled with fear.

Lord, I pray that you would continue to fill my heart with a faith that is firm in you.

Amen.

Let There Be Light

Genesis 1:3 (NIV)
And God said, "Let there be light", and there was light.

Each morning the sun rises and each evening it sets, just as God created it to do.

He colours our skies with shades of red as He shows us the magnificence of His creation.

I was recently away on holidays, and in the town where I was staying, one night per week everyone gathers on the beach and watches as the sun sets over the Indian ocean.

It was an incredible sight to see, and I sat in awe with thousands of others enjoying this beautiful display of God's creation.

After the sun had disappeared from the sky, we were encouraged to clap the sunset in appreciation for the day gone and hope for the promise of a new day to come.

As lovely as these sentiments were, I really wanted to cry out "Let's praise God for the incredible gift He has just shown us". I wanted to stand where I was and openly thank Him for His artwork, and the magnificence of what He had just displayed.

So often as we journey through life, we take the beauty of the world around us for granted, we see the sunrise and sunset, fields of flowers, rugged mountains, and majestic oceans, and as much as we appreciate their beauty, we don't pay homage to their creator. We don't take the time to show reverence to God for the amazing gift of nature, to thank Him for the abundance of colour, or the awesome displays of His power all around us.

In the beginning, God created. He made everything, with a whisper, or a wave of His hand, He brought into being all that we have the privilege of enjoying today.

I would encourage you, next time you can spend time in nature, thank God for all that He has created, all that you see around you, all that you are blessed to be enjoying.

God is the one who brought all these things into being, He is the one who is worthy of our applause, for it is God alone, who is the master craftsman.

Prayer

Father God, I thank you for all you have created, for the day and the night, the sun, the moon and the stars. Every morning as I open my eyes, I look out upon your incredible handiwork, and I am in awe of all you have done.

I pray that I would never tire of expressing my gratitude to you for the beauty that surrounds me. Let me never be more enamoured by the landscape than I am by the landscaper. May I always find time to praise the creator rather than just admire the creation.

Lord, as I spend time in nature, help me to stop and smell the roses, to take time out to truly appreciate my surroundings rather than just rushing through the motions. Lord, help me to slow down and take a breath, to enjoy the crunching leaves, or the rolling waves, may I even enjoy the splashing of rain all around me.

God, whether I stand at the bottom of the mountain, or whether I have trekked to the top, let me see you in it all, in each blade of grass, or craggy rockface, continue to remind me that it was you who brought all of this into being.

Now and forever Lord, I thank you for all that you have made. Amen.

Do Not Be Dismayed

There are times in all our lives when we are afraid. There are times that overwhelm us, and fear becomes our greatest stronghold.

We can be slightly apprehensive, or we can be experiencing full blown terror. It can be anything from being nervous about a job interview, facing the unknown in a hospital bed, not knowing where the money is coming from to feed the family, or fearing the worst with a loved one.

Being afraid, or scared, anxious or fearful can be debilitating. It can keep us up at night, it can leave us breathless, and it can stop us moving forward.

So, where do we go with our fear? What do we do when the reel in our minds won't stop, and we are left in a state of helplessness?

God calls us to give all our burdens over to Him, to let go of all that worries us, and to trust in Him for all our needs, and what we are going through. He wants to stand beside us through every situation, to be our guide on our journey through life, leading us on the paths that He has for us, not necessarily the paths that we choose for ourselves.

He knows that there are some things that we can't possibly carry on our own, there are days that we can't face, and there are situations we are not physically able to walk through alone. God wants to walk with us, He wants to carry our burdens, and to shoulder the weight of all that is pulling us down. It is His greatest desire that we will be in communion with Him, not living in fear alone.

He promises that He will take care of us, He will stay close and protect us during the darkest nights. He will never leave us or forsake us but will stick by us in every situation. He is the only one who can calm our racing hearts and settle the turmoil in our minds.

Today I would encourage you to place your trust in God, hand over your fear, your worries, and your concerns, knowing that He is with you in every situation.

Prayer

Lord Jesus, I come to you with a heart of gratitude for your love, and for your presence of peace in my life. I thank you for the privilege of knowing that you hold me in every situation, and that I have no need to fear when I place my trust in you.

God, you are my safe place, my haven, and my shelter during the ups and downs of life. When everyone else has walked away, you pull me closer.

Lord, I thank you that your perfect love drowns out my deepest fears, that when I keep my eyes focused on you, I take them off all else that would try to consume me. That when my heart is set on you, there is no room for anything else.

God, I place my anxieties, my apprehension, my worries and my concerns into your hands, I ask that you replace each of these emotions with your love, your peace and your provision.

Father, I ask that right now you would fill my mind with only that which is good, pure and true. Help me to fully immerse myself in you, knowing that more of you and less of me is the only way to move forward.

Jesus, I thank you that my greatest fears are where you can do your greatest work, and I would ask you now, Lord, work in me.

Amen.

I Call He Hears

Psalm 61:2 (AMP)
*From the end of the earth I call to You, when my heart is
overwhelmed and weak; Lead me to the rock that is higher than I.*

There are moments in all our lives when we are overwhelmed, when we feel lost, when our world is shaken, and we find ourselves facing situations we never thought we would.

There are days, that can lead to months, or even years, when we feel like we've hit rock bottom, when we feel like the very core of who we are has been stripped away, and we are left with nothing. There are instances where we doubt, we lose faith, we struggle with all we thought we knew, and we find ourselves in a place we simply don't recognise.

In those moments we tend to feel weak, helpless, lost and lonely. Our thoughts are gripped by fear or despair, and we are unsure how to put one foot in front of the other and keep going. It can feel like our journey has ended and we are now just stuck.

Yet, we have hope, we have the promise of help, of safety, and of strength. We are not alone, but we are held by God, the same God who holds the stars in the sky, holds us.

In our darkest moments, God is with us. He leads us and guides us. He protects us, in our body, soul and spirit. We can rest in Him.

He leads us to a place of refuge, a place of shelter, and a place where we are once again restored and renewed, where we can rise on eagle's wings.

All we need to do is call on Him, it doesn't matter where we are, or what we are facing, He has an open ear and loving heart towards us. He will take what is overwhelming us, what is making us weak, and He will transform us.

Our God in His loving kindness leads us to the rock, to Jesus, our hope and our defender. No matter what you are going through today, know that He is with you in all things.

Prayer

Lord, I thank you that you are with me today, that no matter what I face, I don't face it alone, for you are before me and behind me, hedging me in on all sides, and protecting me from all that comes against me.

God, I thank you that you give me courage to stand when I feel like cowering, you strengthen my bones when I feel weak, and when I am in a place of overwhelm you hold me up and help me to keep putting one foot in front of the other.

I thank you for your refuge and shelter, that you are my hiding place and my home. God thank you for standing in the gap, for carrying my burdens and for easing my load. I am so grateful that I can walk into my freedom, knowing that it has already been bought with a price.

Lord, I thank you that the core of who I am is not determined by my circumstances, but rather, by you. I don't have to bow down in weakness, but rather I can stand tall in victory, knowing that the God of today leads me into tomorrow, and that together we walk side by side.

I thank you Lord, that my hope is in you, and that I can rest in the knowledge of this, allowing my heart to be filled with peace as I stand on the truth of your promises. For all of this and more, I give thanks.

Amen.

Embracing Change

There can be times in life when change is welcomed, when we run towards it with open arms, and there are other times when change fills us with fear, dread, and unrest.

Not all of us enjoy new seasons, especially when they are filled with hardship or pain. It can be difficult to embrace change when it comes as a surprise, and not in a good way. But God reminds us in Daniel that He is the author of the changing of seasons, and this means that there is a time for everything, and that includes the good, the bad, the unexpected and the different.

How we react to, and handle change will often heighten or lessen the impact it has on us. When we are given good news, like a promotion, the excitement of a wedding, a baby in the family, or a great holiday, we are often thrilled and full of joy for what is to come. However, when the news is not good, such as illness, the loss of a job, the death of someone close, or the end of a dream, we are filled with despair and find ourselves failing in our ability to cope.

Yet God says there is a season for all things, that means all changes, good and bad, welcomed and not so welcomed will take place. He will determine the rise and fall of leaders, the comings and goings, the full circle of life, and the journey for each of us.

In Ecclesiastes He tells us that there will be weeping and laughing, mourning, and dancing, love and hate, war, and peace. There is nothing left out, no emotion, no aspect of life, no activity, good or bad, we will succumb to it all.

We need to learn to trust in God through all the changes, to place our hope in Him when the seasons are hard, and to rejoice with Him when the seasons are good.

Today I would encourage you to hold onto Him as you walk through the changes in your life, knowing that He will work all things together for your good.

Prayer

Lord, I thank you that you are the God of every season, you are the creator of life, and therefore, you are in all things.

Lord, I thank you that nothing takes place without your knowledge, not a leaf drops from a tree without you knowing about it first.

Every star in the sky is seen by you, and every grain of sand has been carefully placed by your hand.

Lord, you are the author of change, you are the one who opens and closes doors, who provides opportunities and who makes a way where there is no way.

Lord, I hand you this season of my life, and I pray that you have your way. Do as you will for my good and for my benefit. Help me not to resist any change you may have planned for me, but teach me to walk in your ways, leaning not on my own understanding, but trusting wholly in you.

Father God, I thank you that every day of my life, and the lives of those I love is held by you, that you tenderly embrace us and draw us close. I am so grateful that we can rest in who you are, day by day, season by season.

Amen.

A Life Of Service

Psalm 116:12 (NLT)
What can I offer the Lord for all He has done for me?

There is a very famous quote by John F Kennedy, given at his inauguration, in which he says, "Ask not what your country can do for you, but what you can do for your country."

This is the ultimate sign of service and devotion, to not seek out something for ourselves, but to look for ways that we can offer help, render assistance and give back.

In the same way that we seek to offer our service to our family, our community, and our world at large, we too need to give back to God for all that He has done for us. We need to show our gratitude for all that He has graciously given to us.

There is nothing we have that has not been a gift from Him. The very breath in our lungs would not be there had He not first breathed into us. The beauty that we see all around us is His creation, made for our pleasure and enjoyment. He gave His only son that we might be able to enter into relationship with Him, and He daily showers us with His forgiveness, His love and His grace.

The question all of us should ask each day should always be 'Lord, what can I offer you?'

Today, no matter where you are on your journey, I would encourage each of you to find ways to give back to God, either in serving Him, or in serving others because of Him.

Give back with your time, with your finances, with your worship and with your love.

Step out of your comfort zone and offer yourself as a living sacrifice, let all that you do be for His glory and for His honour.

Look for opportunities to reach out to others, to allow God to lead you to those who need a tangible touch from Him, be willing to be His hands and feet to those around you.

In all things, offer all that you are, and all that you have to the God who has given His all for you.

Prayer

Father God, I thank you for who you are, and for all you've given.

I am so grateful for the gift of Jesus, that you would allow your Son to pay my debts, that you would allow Him to die on the cross in my place.

Lord, how can I give back to you? What can I possibly do that is worthy of all that you do for me?

Jesus, open my eyes that I might see the needs around me, lead me by your Spirit to those who need a gentle word, a loving touch, and a helping hand.

Help me to take my eyes off myself and place them on you. Help me to serve willingly, to follow without reservation, and to give back in a way that shows how much I love you.

Father God, help me to be your hands and feet, going where you would have me go, and saying what you would have me say.

Not my will Lord, but yours.

Amen.

Our Firm Foundation

John 14:27 (NIV)

Peace I leave with you, my peace I give you. I do not give to you as the world gives. Do not let your hearts be troubled and do not be afraid.

The world we live in can be an unsettling and frightening place. We are bombarded daily with the images of war, the gory visuals of death and destruction. We are faced with the ugliness of life, the depravity of the human spirit, and the assault to our senses of how low another person can go to gratify their own lustful desires. With all of this happening around us, it is so easy to become overwhelmed and fearful for not only today, but for all of our tomorrows.

It is not hard to fall into the trap of feeling hopeless and to give up believing that good can come from all the bad in the world.

Yet, as Christians, we have the promise of peace. We have the hope of knowing that God is the bigger picture, that He is the victor in this story, and that He will not leave us, to journey alone, but will walk with us through every situation we face, giving us His peace in the storm.

We all face our own battles, we have struggles with our health, our families, our jobs, and our own personal demons. But in and through Him, we don't face these things alone. We can have 'the peace that passes understanding' when we place our faith in God, when we allow Him to be our constant, and when we lean into and trust in Him.

Jesus has told us not to let our hearts be troubled, and not to be afraid. Yet how hard this seems!

But when we can truly grasp who He is, when we realise that the world will never offer us anything that is lasting, anything that we can fully trust in, then we know without a shadow of a doubt, that our only hope can be found in putting our lives into the hands of God and allowing Him to carry us. Allowing Him to be our peace, to be the one who is our firm foundation and the rock on which we stand.

Today I would encourage you to put your trust in Jehovah Shalom, for He is our peace, today, tomorrow and forever.

Prayer

Lord, when all around me is falling away, when my hope seems to be failing and all that I have held dear seems lost, remind me that my peace is in you. Remind me that the world will never calm my fears, will never hold me in the dark, and will never lead me by still waters, all that I need, and desire, can only be found in you.

God, there are days when I feel lost, when the joy of yesterday seems like a distant memory, and the hope of tomorrow may never come, help me to continue to trust in you, knowing that it is you alone who will give me rest and will hold my heart.

Father, when all I see around me fills me with dread and fear, when I can't stop the noise in my head or struggle to fight off the images I see, help me to focus fully on you. Lord, help me to shut down everything else and listen only for your voice, to drown out the crowd so that I might hear your soft whisper.

Lord Jesus, when my faith feels shaky, and I stumble through each day, give me courage to keep going, give me strength to keep fighting, and give me peace to pave the way

Amen.

Come As You Are

Matthew 6:6 (MSG)
Find a quiet secluded place, so you won't be tempted to role play before
God. Just be there as simply and honestly as you can manage. The focus
will shift from you to God, and you will begin to sense His grace.

God wants us to come to Him in prayer just as we are. He doesn't expect a big theatrical encounter, He doesn't expect us to use big words and lengthy sentences, He just wants the real us to come before Him, however that may look.

Sometimes we get caught up in thinking that we need to have it all together, we need to present the 'perfect' us to God. We need to get all our thoughts sorted out and come before Him when we are in a presentable state.

God has never expected that from us, He doesn't want to only hear from us when we have a semi-sorted life, He wants to know us on our good and our bad days. He wants to be with us amidst the ugliness of the journey we are on, whatever we are going through, when we are hurting or depressed, when we are struggling and when we feel like we are completely unlovable.

God wants us to actively pursue Him, He wants us to be under His umbrella of grace, and to live a life of simplicity and honesty before Him.

He asks that we find a quiet place to meet with Him, a place where we won't be distracted, where we won't be tempted to grandstand during our time with Him. He wants us to Himself, not where we are surrounded by others who will steal our attention and pull us away from being in full communion with Him.

Today I would encourage you to give God your whole self; to lay down all you are for Him. Take time out and spend it with Him, both praying and then listening to what He has to say. Find yourself shadowed in the wings of His grace, wholly sold out in who you are for His glory.

Prayer

Lord, I thank you that I can come to you just as I am, with all my faults and failures, warts and all.

Lord God, I am so grateful that you expect nothing from me, that the time I spend with you can be honest and real, you are not expecting me to show up perfectly put together. Thank you that I can come with my tears, with my disappointments, my anger, my hurts and everything in between. There is nothing I need to hide from you, but I can just bring it all.

Lord, you are full of grace and mercy, and I thank you that each day you offer that to me anew, that I can come to you a mess, but can leave refreshed and renewed. You are a God of forgiveness, and when I cry out to you of all that is wrong, you forgive me and make everything right.

Lord Jesus, you are my hope when all hope is lost, and I am so grateful that on the days when I think I can't possibly put one foot in front of the other, it is in those moments that you carry me.

In the words of the hymn by Charlotte Elliott 'Just as I am without one plea', Lord this is my prayer today.

Amen.

God's Plans For You

Jeremiah 29:11 (NIV)
"For I know the plans I have for you," declares the Lord, "plans to
prosper you and not to harm you, plans to give you hope and a future."

This is an incredible verse, it speaks of hope, of promise, and of provision.

The thing I love the most about it is it doesn't say 'I know the plans I have for SOME of you'. It's not just for the odd one or two, it's not for the super spiritual, it's not for those who have it all together. It's for all of us. It's for each of us individually. God has a plan and a purpose for you and for me. His plan includes prosperity, protection and a hopeful future.

God wants us to dream big, He doesn't want us to limit Him to what we think He might do, but He wants us to reach for the sky with what He could do. He is the God of more than enough, the God who can part the sea, who can turn water into wine, who can raise the dead to life. He is not hindered by the smallness of our thinking, but He has plans far above anything we could possibly imagine.

If God calls you into His purpose for your life, it's not so that He can leave you wondering, it's not to trick you or to side swipe you. When God starts showing you His plan it's to prepare you, to get you excited, and to get you on your feet and moving on the journey He has for you. Take that first step with Him, don't doubt His leading or His calling, but listen for His whisper, and lean into all that He is showing you.

Just like the story of Esther, God is going to do mighty things through you. Just because you feel inadequate, doesn't mean that He won't use you, just because you're not sure doesn't mean He won't open doors, and just because you don't have faith in yourself, doesn't mean He doesn't have faith in you.

If God can bring water from a rock, He can most certainly take your life and make something amazing and beautiful from it, He just needs you to be willing and open.

Today I would encourage you, dream big, and see where God takes you.

Prayer

Father, I thank you that you are a loving God who has chosen to lead me into the place you have called me. I thank you that you walk with me, that the plans you have for me are purposeful and will fulfill all your promises for my life.

Lord, as I step into the unknown, as I walk in faith on the journey you have for me, help me to lean not on my own understanding, but to trust fully in you. God even when I can't see what's ahead, when I don't have the full picture, and when I feel apprehensive about what is to come, I thank you that in all this, I can trust in you.

On the days when I feel discouraged, when my head hurts and my heart feels lost, God, even then, help me to remain faithful to your calling, to not give up, but to remain hopeful in that which you have planned for me.

Lord Jesus, you are the rock on which my world is built, help me to stay steadfast, to keep my eyes focused, and to remember each day why I do what I do, not for my glory but for yours.

As I put one foot in front of the other, as I choose to follow your calling, Lord, I thank you that your plan for me will give me a hope and a future, that I need not fear the terror of night, for you keep me safe from all harm.

Father God, I know that as I remain in you, you will remain in me, that you are the vine, you are the way, the truth and the life, and you are the hope of all my tomorrows.

Amen.